THE PREMARITAL PLANNER

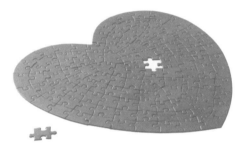

The Premarital Planner

YOUR COMPLETE LEGAL GUIDE TO A PERFECT MARRIAGE

Vikki S. Ziegler, Esq.

FOREWORD BY JUDGE MICHAEL K. DIAMOND (RET.)

imagine! Publishing

Library of Congress Cataloging-in-Publication is available on request

An Imagine Book

Published by Charlesbridge
85 Main Street
Watertown, MA 02472
(617) 926-0329
www.charlesbridge.com

Printed in China

10 9 8 7 6 5 4 3 2 1

Manufactured in January, 2012

ISBN 978-1-936140-68-8

For information about custom editions, special sales, premium
and corporate purchases, please contact Charlesbridge Publishing
at specialsales@charlesbridge.com

TO MY PARENTS

Had it not been for your divorce, I would never have really understood what it takes to be in a healthy, thriving, and loving relationship. Those lessons were life-changing. And I know my purpose.

CONTENTS

HAPPY MARRIAGE RESOURCES

ACKNOWLEDGMENTS

Thank you to all my family, friends, and coworkers who have always believed in me and supported my passion to become an author. Without your love and support my dream could never have come true.

To my beloved parents, Lana and Lewis, thank you for getting divorced! Your divorce set me on the path to a wonderfully fulfilling career that has allowed me to help others in unimaginable ways. Thank you for your relentless support, but most importantly, for always believing in me. I have adopted the best parts of both of you, and for that I am forever grateful.

To Glenn, thank you for always being my cheerleader and someone I could count on, day or night, for brilliant advice.

To Susan, thank you for your friendship, which has become a source of strength for me over the years. To my brother Oren, thank you for teaching me what unconditional love looks like.

To Bill, for your unconditional love and support. You will never know how much I truly appreciate you and what you have taught me! You are my true love.

To Lisa, Lori, Heather, and Karen for always being my Number 1 fans. My love for you is everlasting. You are part of my sisterhood. To Alex, my protégé, my "little Nu." My love for you is indescribable. You are an extraordinary person, friend, and are destined for superstardom. Thank you from the bottom of my heart for all that you have done for me.

To Judge Micky, for being my mentor and allowing me to gain knowledge and insight from a truly remarkable man. I cherish your friendship. To Nancy, for showing me that I have a voice and always believing in me when I didn't believe in myself. Your guidance has changed my life. Thank you, humbly.

To D. Long, for always being there for me day or night. Without you, I would be in BIG trouble. You are an amazing person!

To my all-star team, David Drachman, Charlie Nurnberg, Jeremy Nurnberg, Joanne O'Sullivan, and Cindy LaBreacht. Without your guidance, wisdom, and belief in me this book could never have turned out so well. Thank you for your tireless work and unrelenting belief that I have something to offer couples getting married. You are true professionals, and most importantly, amazing people whom I'm proud to call friends. I am honored to be in your company. David Drachman, you must know you brought this book to life: you are my book hero, and I thank you from the bottom of my heart.

To all my clients, who have dared to show me their true selves and who have allowed me to turn their pain into growth. Each one of you has taught me an invaluable lesson. Without those lessons, this book would not be possible.

I have always wanted to make the people I love proud. It is my sincere hope that this book has accomplished that.

To all my readers, my lesson to you is to learn from my mistakes. You have what it takes to stay in a loving, beautiful marriage forever. Heed my advice and you will be fantastic role models for those around you. Believe in love. Believe in marriage. May you follow love any way you deem fit. But most importantly, may you be happy.

FOREWORD

**"For better or for worse, in sickness
and in health, to love, and honor..."**

When these words are spoken during the marriage ceremony, how many of us really listen and understand the commitment being made? The excitement of the planning, the ceremony, the party afterward, and the honeymoon are on the minds of most happy couples.

After the honeymoon is over and the realities of a marriage commitment set in, the daily stress and pressures of life start to take over, and more than 50 percent of marriages in the US today end in divorce.

Is it because couples get married too young, haven't experienced the pressures of employment or having to pay living expenses for two, etc.? Or is it because couples don't take the time to think about the step they are about to take and don't consider the many and varied planning opportunities available for helping make their marriage survive?

Whether you're wealthy in your own right or struggling to make ends meet, if you're considering getting married today, you should explore the potential obstacles you may face in an effort to eliminate, reduce, or at the very least, minimize them.

The Premarital Planner does exactly that. As a presiding judge in family court for the past 16 years, I've seen and heard just about every story about why marriages don't survive.

Whether it's money issues, stress of employment (or lack thereof), child-rearing, lack of communication, growing apart, or whatever the reason, simple planning and understanding will go a long way toward making your marriage work.

If each of the thousands of couples that appeared before me had the benefit of this book prior to their marriage ceremony, I am convinced that the majority of those marriages could have been saved.

Vikki Ziegler gives you not only the benefit of her insight from years of representing divorcing parties, but also realistic, practical common-sense suggestions on how to thrive in your marriage.

You will find this book informative and sometimes humorous. But most importantly, you'll find in it the key not only to making your marriage survive, but to making your marriage the best years of your life.

Judge Michael K. Diamond (Ret.)

INTRODUCTION

Before her wedding five years ago, Chloe chose not to execute a prenuptial agreement. She was so focused on the wedding, she didn't have time to think much beyond it. And she was in love; convinced her marriage would last forever. With her jet-black hair and bronzed skin, she walked down the aisle in her strapless Vera Wang gown, waving and smiling at the 300 guests there to wish her well in her marriage to Rick. But unfortunately, Chloe didn't get her happy ending.

Sitting in my office with tears streaming down her face, looking drained and gaunt, Chloe begged me for legal advice on how to proceed with her unfortunate divorce. Listening to her story, like so many others, I couldn't help but imagine that it could have turned out differently if the two of them had simply had several important conversations before saying "I do."

While brides and grooms spend countless hours discussing wedding guest lists, flowers, and menus for the reception, few devote significant time to the all-important conversations on issues that will affect their entire married life: finances, children, healthcare, and estate planning. Talking about these topics is not easy. But these kinds of conversations are essential to ensuring a firm foundation for a happy and healthy marriage. So, amidst the wine and roses, how do you bring up the decidedly unromantic topic of life insurance? Prenuptial agreements? Cohabitation agreements? This book is here to help and ease your concerns so that these important topics don't get swept under the rug.

After more than a decade in family law practice, I've worked with financial planners, family therapists, life coaches, and many unhappy couples. Through it all, I've discovered that the keys to a long-lasting marriage are honesty and careful planning. Discussing vital topics such as children, money, family relationships and dynamics, and prior relationships before the wedding will bring you closer to a stronger union. But how do you start?

Using what I've learned over the past decade, I've created this guide to help you sort through the many issues facing modern couples, and to give you tools for discussing them before tying the knot. Some topics are more sensitive than others. Some should come at the beginning of your relationship, others when you've already decided to wed. Starting before the proposal and taking you well into your marriage, I'll guide you step by step through building the strong foundation necessary for your marriage to thrive.

Watching marriages unravel is difficult, but doing so has offered me invaluable insight. I present it to you here, along with interactive charts and tips and tools to help you and your partner strengthen your union. Read *The Premarital Planner* once on your own. Then read it again, this time filling out the exercises and questionnaires. Request that your partner do the same. Share your answers with each other. By doing this, the two of you will come to a greater understanding of each other's perspective on some of the most important issues in your marriage. You'll realize there are always skills you can acquire and ways to improve your relationship. You'll enter the most important relationship in your life on a solid foundation and with a greater chance of success.

Thank you for allowing me to be part of your journey. While your happiness is ultimately up to you, my premarital tips and tools will help you improve your chances of having a healthy, loving marriage that defies odds.

Speak NOW

(or Forever Hold Your Peace)

Before you pop the question, ask and
answer these big questions together

Together.
Forever?

Good fortune is what happens
when opportunity meets planning.
—Thomas Edison

Couples sometimes wait six months to two or three years before they start thinking about marriage. There's no right or wrong answer about when to start your premarital planning; however, my rule of thumb is this: it takes nine months to make a baby—so why not give yourself at least that amount of time to plan your union? Of course, every relationship is unique and you as a couple need to decide when it feels right. But that doesn't mean wait until two weeks before your wedding to start planning! Premarital considerations are vast and detailed: it takes time and commitment to set your marriage up to work so that it lasts.

Thinking about buying a ring, proposing, and asking the bride-to-be's father for permission to wed can be nerve-racking for some, while for others, deciding to wed feels easy and smooth. It really boils down to personality type. Regardless of your approach, once you've determined that you want to be engaged and the feelings are mutual, it's time to set down a romantic time to talk through the premarital tasks at hand. The topics in this book will help organize and highlight the most important areas of marital planning. I tell couples to look at this process as though you are building a home. Each of you has different views on how things should be.

So many couples fail to discuss important topics before they wed and leave them until it's too late. Marriage means more than sharing a bed (and possibly a surname) forever. It means sharing financial responsibilities, making healthcare decisions, and possibly raising children together. And it is a *legal* contract. Not exactly the stuff of romance.

What many starry-eyed lovers don't realize is that if you don't talk about the unromantic stuff in advance, it can lead to many *very* unromantic arguments down the road. This section of *The Premarital Planner* is designed to get you and your partner thinking and talking about yourselves as individuals and as a couple, your hopes and dreams for the future, your habits, and your way of life so that you can make the most informed decisions possible and start the biggest commitment of your life on sound footing.

What I want for you from the onset, even before your engagement, is to make sure you are marrying wisely; that you are not just getting married to get married—that's a surefire way to end up in divorce court. Your goal is to continue in a loving, monogamous relationship for the long haul.

In recent years, there's been a great deal of talk in the media about starter marriages, and a growing acceptance of the idea that if it doesn't work out, you can always just get divorced (see sidebar below). According to recent statistics, one in every 12 couples is heading for the divorce courts after just 24 months of marriage (from "Two Year Itch Infects Marriage," *News Australia*, June 22, 2004). These statistics are staggering.

Marriage should *never* be taken lightly. It is a *very* serious civil commitment. Some view it as a religious union in the eyes of God. Whichever view you hold, make sure you understand the seriousness of the marital contract between you and your partner. Getting married is not the same

SOBERING STATISTICS Marriages are most susceptible to divorce in the early years of marriage. After five years, approximately 10 percent of marriages are expected to end in divorce, and another 10 percent (or 20 percent cumulatively) are divorced by about the tenth year after marriage. However, the 30 percent level is not reached until about the 18th year after marriage, while the 40 percent level is only approached by the 50th year after marriage.

—Rose M. Kreider and Jason M. Fields, "Number, Timing, and Duration of Marriages and Divorces: 1996," U.S. Census Bureau Current Population Reports, February 2002, p. 18.

as getting your driver's license, which can be revoked or suspended. A marital partnership is governed by the laws of the state in which you reside. It's no laughing matter.

Preparing to spend your life with another takes more than wedding planning. It takes a great deal of time and emotional commitment to understand what is required of you in a long-term relationship. Are you ready and willing to make that commitment?

Going through the following quizzes, exercises, and discussions together isn't a legal requirement, but I guarantee that doing so will help you avoid ending up in divorce court.

First Comes Love

Love isn't the only thing that keeps a marriage together, but it's an essential building block. How solid is your love? Start by taking stock of your feelings about your partner. Completing this inventory can be a first step in evaluating your relationship and determining if marriage is really the right move for the two of you. Keep the lists for future reference.

LOVE LISTS

Why Do You Love Your Partner?
List five things below:

1. _____

_____

2. _____

_____

3. _____

_____

4. _____

_____

5. _____

_____

Why Do You Think Your Partner Loves You?
List five things below:

1. _____

_____

2. _____

_____

3. _____

_____

4. _____

_____

5. _____

_____

Just the Two of Us

While you and your partner may truly love each other, there may be issues in your relationship that will affect the success of your marriage. The following questions will help you honestly evaluate where your relationship stands and identify issues that could become critical should you decide to get married.

Take a two-pronged approach when answering the following questions. First, read the questions privately, answering them by yourself and taking the time to think them through thoroughly. Answer honestly and openly: you're only cheating yourself if you breeze through without giving the questions your honest and undivided attention.

Next, share these questions with your partner. Let your partner read and answer them privately. Then compare your responses with your partner and begin a discussion, or revisit one that you have hopefully already had.

Don't just let these questions—and your answers—die on the page. They were meant to be living, vital subjects for you and your partner to share.

OUR RELATIONSHIP: WHERE WE ARE NOW?

1. How solid is your relationship right now?

MY RESPONSE _____

_____

_____

YOUR RESPONSE _____

_____

_____

2. How often do you experience relationship flare-ups or fights?

MY RESPONSE _____

_____

_____

YOUR RESPONSE _____

_____

_____

3. How do you handle those flare-ups and fights?

MY RESPONSE _____

_____

_____

YOUR RESPONSE _____

_____

_____

4. Have you resolved past relationship issues so that you can move forward in building a healthy relationship?

MY RESPONSE _____

_____

_____

YOUR RESPONSE _____

_____

_____

5. Is violence (physical, emotional, or mental) ever an issue in your relationship? If so, how is it handled?

MY RESPONSE _____

_____

_____

YOUR RESPONSE _____

_____

_____

6. Do your arguments ever make you think your partner has "anger issues?"

MY RESPONSE _____

_____

_____

YOUR RESPONSE _____

_____

_____

7. How do you show your partner that he or she is your top priority?

MY RESPONSE _____

_____

_____

YOUR RESPONSE _____

_____

_____

8. How often do you talk openly and honestly with each other?
Is it enough for you?

MY RESPONSE _____

_____

_____

YOUR RESPONSE _____

_____

_____

9. On a scale of 1 to 10 (10 being the best), how would you rate the
quality of your conversations? Why?

MY RESPONSE _____

_____

_____

YOUR RESPONSE _____

_____

_____

10. What have you done, specifically, to build your relationship this week? What has your partner done?

MY RESPONSE _____

_____

_____

YOUR RESPONSE _____

_____

_____

11. What qualities first drew you to your partner?

MY RESPONSE _____

_____

_____

YOUR RESPONSE _____

_____

_____

12. What needs are you trying to meet through your relationship? Is your partner meeting these needs?

MY RESPONSE _____

_____

_____

YOUR RESPONSE _____

_____

_____

13. What issues from your past do you have to resolve in order to ensure that your current relationship does not suffer?

MY RESPONSE _____

_____

_____

YOUR RESPONSE _____

_____

_____

14. What would your partner say you need to change for your relationship to improve?

MY RESPONSE _____

_____

_____

YOUR RESPONSE _____

_____

_____

15. What qualities does your partner have that you lack?

MY RESPONSE _____

_____

_____

YOUR RESPONSE _____

_____

_____

Fully Committed

You love each other, you get along. That's a great start. But you can't build a successful marriage without commitment. With your partner, take this quiz to assess what commitment in a relationship means to each of you.

FULLY COMMITTED QUESTIONNAIRE

1. How important is commitment in this relationship?
   Do you think we feel the same way about it, or do you think we have differing levels of commitment?

   MY RESPONSE _____

   _____

   YOUR RESPONSE _____

   _____

2. List five signs that show I'm committed to you.

   MY RESPONSE _____

   _____

   _____

   _____

   _____

YOUR RESPONSE _____

_____

_____

_____

_____

3. List five signs that show you're committed to me.

MY RESPONSE _____

_____

_____

_____

_____

YOUR RESPONSE _____

_____

_____

_____

_____

4. Have you ever felt this committed in a relationship before? Why or why not?

MY RESPONSE _____

_____

YOUR RESPONSE _____

_____

5. Assess each partner's answer to Question 4.
   Do the answers seem honest?

   MY RESPONSE _____

   _____

   YOUR RESPONSE _____

   _____

6. How would you rate your current level of commitment?
   Do you think we each have an equal level?

   MY RESPONSE _____

   _____

   YOUR RESPONSE _____

   _____

7. How will you plan ahead for staying committed in our marriage?

   MY RESPONSE _____

   _____

   YOUR RESPONSE _____

   _____

8. What factors might violate your commitment to me?

   MY RESPONSE _____

   _____

   YOUR RESPONSE _____

   _____

9. What factors do you think might violate my commitment to you?

MY RESPONSE _____

_____

YOUR RESPONSE _____

_____

10. Is there something you need to tell me now (before tying the knot) about your feelings toward commitment?

MY RESPONSE _____

_____

YOUR RESPONSE _____

_____

LOVE POINTERS

❥ Your past is your past! Use the lessons you've learned from your past relationships, but don't allow them to be a third party in your present relationship.

❥ Temptations will always be out there. Take stock of your willingness to be in a committed relationship.

❥ Fear of making a permanent commitment is the surest way to end your relationship before it even begins.

❥ Outline any trust issues that you and your partner have *before* tying the knot and continue to work on being in a secure relationship.

Breadwinner, Caretaker, Homemaker

ROLES AND EXPECTATIONS IN YOUR MARRIAGE

Roles and expectations are created and defined when two people enter into a romantic relationship, and they begin to change and modify as the partnership grows. Expectations may be based on previous relationships, family dynamics, or images picked up from the media. Those images in particular can lead to unrealistic beliefs that can contribute to dissatisfaction in a marriage. If you're expecting your partner to leave rose petals on the bed, run your bath water every night, and cook breakfast for you on the weekends, you're bound to be disappointed at some point.

According to studies by the National Healthy Marriage Resource Center, expectations of traditional gender roles and behaviors in the US have dramatically changed for both men and women. Men were once seen as autonomous, powerful, controlling, assertive, aggressive, and self-determined. Women were traditionally seen as caregivers and homemakers. Recent research shows a dramatic departure from this view. A survey conducted in 2007, by Amato, Booth, Johnson and Rogers, revealed that by the end of the 1990s, the majority of husbands believed that spouses should share breadwinning, that a wife's employment does not interfere with her role as a mother, and that husbands should take on a greater share of the housework when their wives were employed. The majority of wives expected husbands to perform a greater share of the household chores and childcare. Regardless of whether you're marrying a person of the same gender or the opposite, you should still be able to create your own roles and expectations within your family dynamic, despite tradition. A role defines how you and your partner handle responsibilities, assume leadership on an emotional and financial level, divide household tasks, and parent together. In marriage, there should be a general agreement about who's going to do which tasks on a daily basis. So, what is your role in your relationship? Have you discussed with your partner who's going to pay the bills? Who's going to be in charge of all of the finances and investments? Who will care for the children (if you have them)?

It's important that you and your partner discuss how you were raised so each of you can understand the other's background and how your belief system was created. In traditional or religious households, the expectations are often that people get married at a young age, and that men and women should stick to traditional gender roles. Did your mother take care of the needs of the household while your father went out to work? Or was it the opposite? If both of your parents worked, were you left alone or with older siblings to take care of you? If you were unhappy with the way your parents handled things, it's likely that you'll want your own marriage to be different.

It's important to respect and value the changes that happen as you and your spouse grow through the years. Your partner might intend to stay at home, but later wish to get back into the workforce. Each of us is an ever-evolving individual. Aging, maturing, changes in income, and circumstances, such as the birth of a child, ensure that a couple's roles and expectations are constantly in flux. It's critical to acknowledge the roles that you're currently playing and the expectations that you share for your future roles. It's possible that both you and your partner have different thoughts on how you should be progressing as individuals and as a couple.

Carefully review the following questionnaire to determine how you and your partner define your roles and what you want from each other in the future.

THE ROLE OF A LIFETIME QUESTIONNAIRE

1. What roles do you currently play in our relationship (i.e. provider, homemaker, disciplinarian, good cop, bad cop)?

MY RESPONSE _____

_____

_____

YOUR RESPONSE _____

_____

_____

2. Are you comfortable with your role?

MY RESPONSE _____

_____

_____

YOUR RESPONSE _____

_____

_____

3. Are you comfortable with my role?

MY RESPONSE _____

_____

_____

YOUR RESPONSE _____

_____

_____

4. Do you see these roles staying the same or evolving during the course of our marriage?

MY RESPONSE _____

_____

_____

YOUR RESPONSE _____

_____

_____

5. What role would you prefer to play? Why?

MY RESPONSE _____

_____

_____

YOUR RESPONSE _____

_____

_____

6. What role would you prefer me to play? Why?

MY RESPONSE _____

_____

_____

YOUR RESPONSE _____

_____

_____

7. What expectations do you have of me regarding our roles together?

MY RESPONSE _____

_____

_____

YOUR RESPONSE _____

_____

_____

8. How will you communicate these expectations?

MY RESPONSE _____

_____

_____

YOUR RESPONSE _____

_____

_____

9. Is either of us too controlling?

MY RESPONSE _____

_____

_____

YOUR RESPONSE _____

_____

_____

10. How would you change roles if you could for a day, month, or year?

MY RESPONSE _____

_____

_____

YOUR RESPONSE _____

_____

_____

You, Me, and Everything We Owe

PLANNING YOUR FINANCIAL LIFE

Many couples talk about religion, sex, where they want to live, and what they're going to name their future children. However, perhaps because it's uncomfortable, they never broach the subject of money. Ironically, money and finances are often at the very heart of many failed marriages. There's no research that points to financial problems as the foremost cause of divorce, but they're certainly a stress factor that burdens a relationship and causes unnecessary turmoil between two people. Discussing the union of two financial lives is imperative to having a healthy marriage. The day you wed, your marriage becomes a financial and legal partnership.

Marriage is akin to a business partnership in which both parties have input with respect to the day-to-day finances and future of the business. If each partner is not fully invested, a business cannot be successful and thrive. Before tying the knot, you and your partner must make sure that you are financially compatible and have a similar mindset as it relates to financial matters. Each of you must disclose the entire scope of your financial circumstances, including assets, debts, and liabilities. Furthermore, it's critical that you discuss your salaries, income from all sources, loans, inheritances, savings, credit card debt and credit history, personal and marital financial goals, your monthly budgets, and all other aspects that will affect your marriage and your financial outlook. It can be difficult to come together from a financial perspective, especially if partners have been brought up in families with different economic perspectives. Discuss your background and history and come to a financial compromise as to how you will save, invest, and spend over the course of your marriage.

Things change during a marriage. One spouse may stop working or the other may receive a financial windfall or make a lot of money. Because of this, you'll have to evaluate your financial outlook on an ongoing basis. But before you marry, there must be an agreed-upon underlying mindset. If one partner overspends while the other is being too frugal, it's not going to work. There has to be some middle ground so you, as a couple, can have short-term and long-term plans for financial health.

Before getting married, talk about your spending habits. You may love to travel and your partner may want to go on golf outings every other month. If that's built into your budget and is acceptable to each partner, then you can do it. Budgeting is really about making sure that you're living within your means and saving, but also having fun and enjoying life. Spend intelligently, save as much as possible, and live life to the fullest. As long as you and your spouse can agree on most of the financial terms surrounding your wealth building you will have an easy financial marriage.

Remember, "money can't buy you love." When you're choosing your partner, love, not money, must be the main attraction. But also remember that financial incompatibility can cause severe disruption and truly lead to a dead-end marriage. Here are some money rules that every couple should live by at the outset to ensure financial harmony.

THE FIVE RULES OF MARITAL MONEY MATTERS

1. Air out your financial laundry—the good, the bad, the ugly, and everything in between. No secrets. You don't want to find any financial land mines after you're married.

2. Hold monthly meetings to review your finances and discuss adjusting your savings, spending, and budget.

3. Make investing fun for the both of you. Designate one person to look for new ways of investing. When one spouse focuses on the

way to help your marital money grow, the other can learn and discuss his or her feelings about the investment goals and strategies. You don't need a business degree from Harvard to maintain interest in your family's financial future. Intuition, common sense, and trust will go a long way toward making your money work for your marriage.

4. Never make financial assumptions. Ask questions and talk about money. Ask permission from your partner to buy an extravagant gift or to book a trip to Europe. Compromise about money. Put needs and priorities before wants. Develop a mature attitude about finances from the outset.

5. Create realistic expectations about money. Know what you can and can't afford.

THE PREMARITAL MONEY QUESTIONNAIRE

1. What are your financial goals?

MY RESPONSE _____

_____

_____

YOUR RESPONSE _____

_____

_____

2. Where do you see yourself financially in five years? In ten years?

MY RESPONSE _____

_____

YOUR RESPONSE _____

_____

3. What is your FICO score? Do you know my score?

MY RESPONSE _____

_____

_____

YOUR RESPONSE _____

_____

_____

4. What are your feelings about money, in terms of spending it,
   saving it, having it, or wanting it?
   Would you classify yourself as a saver or as a spender?

MY RESPONSE _____

_____

_____

YOUR RESPONSE _____

_____

_____

5. What is your current monthly budget?
   Do you have any net income to put into savings or investments
   after you pay your monthly bills? If so, how much?

MY RESPONSE _____

_____

_____

YOUR RESPONSE _____

_____

_____

6. How often do we communicate about finances?
What is the typical outcome of these communications?

MY RESPONSE _____

_____

_____

YOUR RESPONSE _____

_____

_____

7. If one of us lost a job, could we adjust our budget without creating more debt?

MY RESPONSE _____

_____

_____

YOUR RESPONSE _____

_____

_____

8. How do you feel about borrowing money from others?
Do you owe money to friends or family?
If so, how much and what are the terms of repayment?

MY RESPONSE _____

_____

_____

YOUR RESPONSE _____

_____

_____

9. Do you plan on keeping an individual bank account during our marriage?

MY RESPONSE _____

_____

_____

YOUR RESPONSE _____

_____

_____

10. Can you describe your spending habits and how they differ from mine?

MY RESPONSE _____

_____

_____

YOUR RESPONSE _____

_____

_____

11. Will all of our bank records be sent to our home each month?

MY RESPONSE _____

_____

_____

YOUR RESPONSE _____

_____

_____

12. Where will we keep our important records?

MY RESPONSE _____

_____

_____

YOUR RESPONSE _____

_____

_____

13. Who will be in charge of filing all-important records/documents such as taxes, life insurance, mortgage documents, and our will?

MY RESPONSE _____

_____

_____

YOUR RESPONSE _____

_____

_____

14. If we inherited or won $5 million, what would you want to do with our winnings? Would you want to give some to friends, family, charities, or save for our future?

MY RESPONSE _____

_____

_____

YOUR RESPONSE _____

_____

_____

THE CASH QUESTIONNAIRE

1. What is the current value of your savings account, including balance, interest rate, and any monthly income?

   MY RESPONSE _____

   _____

   _____

   YOUR RESPONSE _____

   _____

   _____

2. What is the current value of your checking account, including balance, interest rate, and any monthly income?

   MY RESPONSE _____

   _____

   _____

   YOUR RESPONSE _____

   _____

   _____

3. What is the current value of your money market accounts, including balance, interest rate, and any monthly income?

   MY RESPONSE _____

   _____

   _____

   YOUR RESPONSE _____

   _____

   _____

4. What is the value of any other miscellaneous accounts not already accounted for, including balance, interest rate, and any monthly income?

MY RESPONSE _____

_____

_____

YOUR RESPONSE _____

_____

_____

5. Do you have income from any other sources, including parents or other family, or under-the-table income?

MY RESPONSE _____

_____

_____

YOUR RESPONSE _____

_____

_____

MARITAL INVESTMENT WORKSHEET

ACCOUNT TYPES & NUMBERS	PURCHASE PRICE	CURRENT VALUE	INTEREST RATE	MATURITY INCOME	MONTHLY INCOME	LOCATION OF DOCUMENT
Mutual Funds						
Stocks						
Bonds						
Annuities						

RETIREMENT ACCOUNT ASSETS WORKSHEET

ACCOUNT TYPES & NUMBERS	CURRENT VALUE	RETURN	COMPANY MATCH	MONTHLY INCOME	LOCATION OF DOCUMENT
IRA (specify Roth or traditional)					
KEOGH					
401(K)					
403(B)					
TSA					
OTHER					
Are you eligible to receive a pension?					
Do you have any loans against your present retirement plan?					

CREDIT CARD DEBTS AND LOANS WORKSHEET

	MY RESPONSE	YOUR RESPONSE
CREDIT CARD	_____	_____
Amount Owed	_____	_____
Interest Rate	_____	_____
Annual Fee	_____	_____
SCHOOL LOAN	_____	_____
Amount owed	_____	_____
Interest rate	_____	_____
Annual fee	_____	_____
CAR LOAN	_____	_____
Amount owed	_____	_____
Financial term of loan	_____	_____
Monthly payment	_____	_____
PERSONAL LOAN	_____	_____
Amount owed	_____	_____
Interest rate	_____	_____
Annual fee	_____	_____
PROMISSORY NOTE	_____	_____
THIRD-PARTY NOTE/DEBT	_____	_____
MORTGAGE	_____	_____
Amount owed	_____	_____
Interest rate/term	_____	_____
Name on liability	_____	_____

FINANCIAL PLANNING QUESTIONNAIRE

1. Do you have a certified financial planner? If so, who is it, and will we join our assets together?

   Can we schedule and keep quarterly meetings with that individual? Can we put together a questionnaire to bring to the meeting?

   MY RESPONSE _____

   _____

   _____

   _____

   YOUR RESPONSE _____

   _____

   _____

   _____

2. Do you have a Certified Public Accountant (CPA)? If so, who is it? Can we make an appointment with this individual to make sure that we are both familiar with our tax advantages once we are married?

   MY RESPONSE _____

   _____

   _____

   _____

   YOUR RESPONSE _____

   _____

   _____

   _____

3. Do you have a stockbroker?

If so, who is it?

Can we make an appointment with this individual, so that we can make joint financial decisions together with the advice of this investor or broker?

MY RESPONSE _____

_____

_____

YOUR RESPONSE _____

_____

_____

MARITAL SPENDING QUESTIONNAIRE

1. Who should write out the checks for our monthly bills?

MY RESPONSE _____

_____

YOUR RESPONSE _____

_____

2. Who will balance our checkbook and file all of the documents that we receive on a monthly basis?

MY RESPONSE _____

_____

YOUR RESPONSE _____

_____

3. How much debt do we each owe?

   How do we intend to pay it down each month?

   From which account will you pay down your debt?

MY RESPONSE _____

_____

_____

YOUR RESPONSE _____

_____

_____

4. Who will buy gifts for our friends' and family members' birthdays and holidays?

MY RESPONSE _____

_____

_____

YOUR RESPONSE _____

_____

_____

5. How much will we spend on luxury items, such as jewelry, sporting events, plays, and vacations?

MY RESPONSE _____

_____

_____

YOUR RESPONSE _____

_____

_____

6. When shopping, do you like to hunt for a bargain, or would you rather pay full price?

MY RESPONSE _____

_____

_____

YOUR RESPONSE _____

_____

_____

7. Do you believe in tithing? If so, what percentage of your income or of our income in the future, should be donated?
To which nonprofits do you contribute?

MY RESPONSE _____

_____

_____

YOUR RESPONSE _____

_____

_____

8. Do you have a will? If not, do you believe it is necessary that a will be drafted as soon as possible?

MY RESPONSE _____

_____

_____

YOUR RESPONSE _____

_____

_____

9. What are your money dreams? If you had unlimited funds, what
would you want to do with them?

MY RESPONSE _____

_____

_____

YOUR RESPONSE _____

_____

_____

Marital Assets

Now that you have answered all questions in the previous section, list
your current assets. Current assets should include anything of value that
is owned by you, or was gifted to you, including any cash that you have,
inventory (if you own a business), short-term investments, marketable
securities, CD's, stocks and bonds, and savings accounts. All figures
should be based on current market value. Decide what will remain separate and what you will combine. These are tough but necessary decisions
that must be made.

CURRENT ASSETS

	ME	YOU
CASH	_____	_____
	_____	_____
	_____	_____
SAFETY DEPOSIT BOX	_____	_____
	_____	_____
	_____	_____

BANK ACCOUNTS

Type   _____   _____

Account Title   _____   _____

Account #   _____   _____

Value   _____   _____

Date of Value   _____   _____

Type   _____   _____

Account Title   _____   _____

Account #   _____   _____

Value   _____   _____

Date of Value   _____   _____

Type   _____   _____

Account Title   _____   _____

Account #   _____   _____

Value   _____   _____

Date of Value   _____   _____

Type   _____   _____

Account Title   _____   _____

Account #   _____   _____

Value   _____   _____

Date of Value   _____   _____

Type   _____   _____

Account Title   _____   _____

Account #   _____   _____

Value   _____   _____

Date of Value   _____   _____

Type   _____   _____

Account Title   _____   _____

Account #   _____   _____

Value   _____   _____

Date of Value   _____   _____

INVESTMENTS

Type _____   _____

Account Title _____   _____

Account # _____   _____

Value _____   _____

Date of Value _____   _____

Type _____   _____

Account Title _____   _____

Account # _____   _____

Value _____   _____

Date of Value _____   _____

Type _____   _____

Account Title _____   _____

Account # _____   _____

Value _____   _____

Date of Value _____   _____

Type _____   _____

Account Title _____   _____

Account # _____   _____

Value _____   _____

Date of Value _____   _____

Type _____   _____

Account Title _____   _____

Account # _____   _____

Value _____   _____

Date of Value _____   _____

Type _____   _____

Account Title _____   _____

Account # _____   _____

Value _____   _____

Date of Value _____   _____

RETIREMENT PLANS

Type _____ _____

Account Title _____ _____

Account # _____ _____

Value _____ _____

Date of Value _____ _____

Type _____ _____

Account Title _____ _____

Account # _____ _____

Value _____ _____

Date of Value _____ _____

Type _____ _____

Account Title _____ _____

Account # _____ _____

Value _____ _____

Date of Value _____ _____

Type _____ _____

Account Title _____ _____

Account # _____ _____

Value _____ _____

Date of Value _____ _____

Type _____ _____

Account Title _____ _____

Account # _____ _____

Value _____ _____

Date of Value _____ _____

Type _____ _____

Account Title _____ _____

Account # _____ _____

Value _____ _____

Date of Value _____ _____

LIFE INSURANCE

Amount   _____   _____

Beneficiary   _____   _____

Type   _____   _____

Cash Surrender Value   _____   _____

Date   _____   _____

Amount   _____   _____

Beneficiary   _____   _____

Type   _____   _____

Cash Surrender Value   _____   _____

Date   _____   _____

Amount   _____   _____

Beneficiary   _____   _____

Type   _____   _____

Cash Surrender Value   _____   _____

Date   _____   _____

Amount   _____   _____

Beneficiary   _____   _____

Type   _____   _____

Cash Surrender Value   _____   _____

Date   _____   _____

TRUSTS

Name   _____   _____

Value   _____   _____

Income Received   _____   _____

Date   _____   _____

Name   _____   _____

Value   _____   _____

Income Received   _____   _____

Date   _____   _____

DISABILITY INSURANCE

Amount   _____   _____

Term   _____   _____

REAL ESTATE

Address   _____   _____

Fair Market Value   _____   _____

Down Payment   _____   _____

Address   _____   _____

Fair Market Value   _____   _____

Down Payment   _____   _____

VEHICLES

Make   _____   _____

Model   _____   _____

Purchase Price   _____   _____

Value   _____   _____

Lease   _____   _____

Make   _____   _____

Model   _____   _____

Purchase Price   _____   _____

Value   _____   _____

Lease   _____   _____

Make   _____   _____

Model   _____   _____

Purchase Price   _____   _____

Value   _____   _____

Lease   _____   _____

A Place to Call Home

You and your partner may already be living together (see page 83) and might have a good idea about each other's lifestyle preferences. If not, you'll need to examine and compare your preferences to determine where you'll live. Are you urban people who prefer to walk everywhere? Or would you rather be in the suburbs where you can conveniently commute to work? Do you dream of a big house with a lawn, or can you see yourself in a more rural area surrounded by acres of land? While the location of your home may not seem like an issue to you now, it may become one as the years pass. Life and employment opportunities may take you away from the place where you're currently living. You may have to decide whether or not it's worth it to move for a job, which might mean leaving your family and friends behind.

Deciding how much of your monthly income will go into your mortgage or rent will be another important decision. For some, a house is simply a shelter, not a reflection of self-worth or status, and therefore not worth a bigger percentage of the monthly budget. For others, the appearance of having a nice home or living in the right neighborhood can be very important. Do you know where your partner stands on these issues?

Many married couples buy their first home together. If you believe you'll do so, where will you get the down payment? Will you each contribute equally? Will your parents or your partner's parents contribute?

If you and your partner decide to have children, you may find yourselves wanting to be close to family so that they can help. If so, whose family? This may end up being more of a source of tension than you ever imagined.

Before getting married, it's wise to have a discussion on these fundamental issues. Take the following quiz together to facilitate discussion.

HOUSE AND HOME QUESTIONNAIRE

1. Where do you want to live?

MY RESPONSE _____

_____

YOUR RESPONSE _____

_____

2. Do you want a small or big house?

MY RESPONSE _____

_____

YOUR RESPONSE _____

_____

3. How do you expect we will divide monthly payments? Who will pay and from what account? Direct deposit or checking account?

MY RESPONSE _____

_____

YOUR RESPONSE _____

_____

4. How much debt do you want to incur on a home?

MY RESPONSE _____

_____

YOUR RESPONSE _____

_____

5. Together, how much money can we put down to purchase a home?

MY RESPONSE _____

_____

YOUR RESPONSE _____

_____

6. Where will we get the funds to finance the purchase of a home?

MY RESPONSE _____

_____

YOUR RESPONSE _____

_____

7. What type of mortgage will we apply for upon purchasing?

MY RESPONSE _____

_____

YOUR RESPONSE _____

_____

8. What are your feelings about taking out a second mortgage on our home?

MY RESPONSE _____

_____

YOUR RESPONSE _____

_____

9. What if we must refinance?

MY RESPONSE _____

_____

YOUR RESPONSE _____

_____

10. How would you feel if a family member was sick and needed a place to live?

MY RESPONSE _____

_____

YOUR RESPONSE _____

_____

11. Do you have homeowner's insurance? For how much?
    What is covered on the policy?
    Where is this document located?

MY RESPONSE _____

_____

YOUR RESPONSE _____

_____

12. Would you consider adding an extra mortgage payment each year to reduce our debt more quickly?

MY RESPONSE _____

_____

YOUR RESPONSE _____

_____

In Sickness
and in Health

Traditional wedding vows usually include the line "in sickness and in health," and "till death do us part." These vows are meant to remind the soon-to-be married couple that, although they might be young and healthy at the time of their wedding, life may bring unexpected turns. Although you'd prefer not to think about it, prolonged illnesses, or even the death of you or your spouse, are possibilities for which you must prepare.

As a married couple, you need to consider your plan of action should one of you become unable to speak for yourself. You should be clear about each other's wishes if a situation should occur where either of you needs to be put on life support. You may *think* you know the answers, but it's important to be absolutely certain and get those wishes down in writing. If you're in a same-sex relationship, you'll need to find out about the laws in your state regarding advance medical directives. If your partner were to pass away, do you know about his or her life insurance policies? Are you the beneficiary?

These can be difficult topics for young, healthy people to discuss, but it will only be more difficult should a situation arise that catches you unprepared. We've all heard stories about feuds between families and spouses, each claiming to know what the person in question would have wanted. While not statistically likely to occur, you must prepare to make important decisions for a loved one if he or she becomes incapable of doing so. This is even truer for a couple planning on having children. Make those decisions now, and a potentially painful situation will be that much less painful.

First, you'll want to ensure that your assets pass to your spouse and not other family members. In the absence of proper estate planning, state law could decide where assets pass, and some states laws do not provide for 100 percent of the estate of a decedent (person who dies) to pass to the surviving spouse. For example, the state of New York dictates that a surviving spouse inherits the first $50,000 plus one half of the balance, with the other half passing to the children. Connecticut has a similar rule in cases in which a decedent is survived by a spouse and issue (child). However, if a Connecticut decedent is survived by a spouse and a parent but no children, the surviving spouse gets the first $100,000 and three-quarters of the remainder, with the other one-quarter passing to the decedent's parents!

There are two additional documents that are integral to the foundation estate plan: a living will and a power of attorney. Through a living will, a person typically states that he or she does not want to be kept alive by artificial means, but rather to be made comfortable. A living will usually also contains a healthcare proxy, where a person names someone to make healthcare decisions if he or she is unable to do so.

If a person does not have a living will, his or her loved ones would be required to file a guardianship action in court to obtain control over a sick loved one. While the expense and delay caused by an application to the court is bad enough, there is no way to guarantee that the court will appoint the person you want to make these decisions for you. Recall the famous case of Terri Schiavo, who suffered brain damage resulting from cardiac arrest, leaving her in a persistent vegetative state. Her husband and parents fought in court for more than seven years to determine who would be her legal guardian. A living will eliminates the expense and heartache for loved ones by stating your wishes with respect to artificial life support and medical decisions. Every person 18 years or older should have one. This is extremely important for a married person, since there can be competing opinions between a person's spouse and other family members.

A power of attorney, on the other hand, controls your property decisions while you're alive. If you become unable to make decisions about your assets, you can name somebody as attorney-in-fact to make such decisions for you. For example, if you were hospitalized after a car accident, you may not be able to attend to your financial affairs, such as paying bills, etc. If a power of attorney is not in place, your loved ones would be required to apply to the court to be named guardian of the property. The same issues apply here as with a living will—namely, there is delay, expense, and, most unfortunately, the possibility the court may not name a guardian you would have chosen. This hardship can be avoided by the implementation of a power of attorney.

According to attorney Brad Shalit, one important consideration relating to a power of attorney is whether it should be durable or springing. A durable power of attorney is effective immediately, whereas a springing power of attorney only becomes effective when the principal is incapacitated. The idea is that the principal may not want the attorney-in-fact to have control over his or her financial affairs until the time that he or she becomes incapacitated. The springing power of attorney might require written statements from two physicians before the attorney-in-fact is able to act for the principal. While this affords protection to the principal's assets, it can be cumbersome and difficult to prove to a financial institution that the principal is truly incapacitated. Moreover, financial institutions can be resistant to accepting a springing power of attorney for fear of potential liability.

The durable power of attorney, on the other hand, is effective immediately and is not affected by the principal's lack of capacity. However, a problem arises when an attorney-in-fact uses the power of attorney for unauthorized acts. The obvious way to avoid this is to name only trustworthy individuals attorneys-in-fact. There may be cases where there isn't a reliable choice, or a principal may not trust anyone. In these instances, one may consider leaving the durable power of attorney to his or her attorney to hold in escrow. The attorney would be instructed to release the power of attorney to the attorney-in-fact upon the attorney's determination that the principal is actually incapacitated.

Most important to young parents is the question of who will take care of their children if both parents die while the children are minors. If the parents do not designate whom they desire to serve as guardian of their minor children, the courts make this decision. Here, it could be more likely that each parent's families could fight over who will be named as guardian of the minor children. A proper will can name guardians for minor children. This is another important decision that most parents would most likely want to make themselves, as opposed to having a judge make the choice.

People often want to name a sibling and his or her spouse as guardians for minor children. The potential problem is that if your sister and her husband are named as guardians, but subsequently get divorced, the minor children may be dragged into a custody battle. Therefore, a practical alternative can be to name the sister as guardian and then, if the sister is serving as guardian but subsequently cannot serve, her husband will since he's already serving the father's role.

It's important to work with an attorney to put your wishes in writing. If you don't have a will, have one prepared, and if you do, make sure that it's amended to reflect your changed wishes should you and your partner get married. Make sure you know about each other's life insurance policies, and if you don't have any, consider arranging to buy some. Take the following quiz to guide your discussion.

INSURANCE POLICIES QUESTIONNAIRE

1. Do you have a life insurance policy?

MY RESPONSE _____

YOUR RESPONSE _____

Where are these documents located?

MY RESPONSE _____

YOUR RESPONSE _____

If so, who is the beneficiary of this policy?

MY RESPONSE _____

YOUR RESPONSE _____

What is the value of this policy?

MY RESPONSE _____

YOUR RESPONSE _____

Is it Term or Whole?

MY RESPONSE _____

YOUR RESPONSE _____

Do you own an annuity?

MY RESPONSE _____

YOUR RESPONSE _____

Value?

MY RESPONSE _____

YOUR RESPONSE _____

Beneficiary?

MY RESPONSE _____

YOUR RESPONSE _____

2. Do you have health insurance?

MY RESPONSE _____

YOUR RESPONSE _____

If so, through what company?

MY RESPONSE _____

YOUR RESPONSE _____

Where are the documents located?

MY RESPONSE _____

YOUR RESPONSE _____

What costs do you incur to have this policy?

MY RESPONSE _____

YOUR RESPONSE _____

Can you add a spouse to your policy?

MY RESPONSE _____

YOUR RESPONSE _____

If so, what is the cost to add a spouse?

MY RESPONSE _____

YOUR RESPONSE _____

3. Do you receive any type of social security or disability benefits? If so, please describe.

MY RESPONSE _____

_____

YOUR RESPONSE _____

_____

4. Do you have disability insurance? If so, for how much?

MY RESPONSE _____

YOUR RESPONSE _____

What are the terms?

MY RESPONSE _____

YOUR RESPONSE _____

Where is this document located?

MY RESPONSE _____

YOUR RESPONSE _____

And Baby Makes Three?

Have you been dreaming of the day when you can throw the football around with Junior? Have you fantasized about dressing up your little girl in a pink dress with a bow? Do you dream about pushing a stroller, or do the thoughts of 3:00 a.m. feedings and dirty diapers make you cringe? Have you shared these thoughts and feelings with your partner? How does your partner really feel about children? Have you ever discussed this very important issue? Many couples, especially early on in a relationship, fail to take the topic of having children seriously. Leaving the subject of whether or not to have children for post-marriage discussions can be a very dangerous decision. The desire for a child is something uniquely personal to each individual. Male or female, every person feels differently about being a parent. It's a very important topic that must be addressed in a serious way.

Children change the dynamic of a relationship as soon as they come into the picture. It's important for you and your partner to discuss whether or not you're ready to bring children into this world—on an emotional level and a financial one. Your life belongs to your child the minute he or she is welcomed into your world. You both have to be able and willing to share your time and love and affection with a child and try to handle all the changes that come along with parenthood.

First, couples should discuss any medical conditions that may impede the normal method of conceiving and/or any known genetic conditions. It's important to also discuss adoption, foster care, and surrogacy if an alternate route to starting your family might be necessary.

If you want a child and your partner doesn't, this could be a deal breaker. Many enter a marriage convinced that a partner will eventually change his or her mind about children after they're married and a few years have passed. While that's a possibility, and no one can predict the future, making that assumption is taking a big gamble.

Once the two of you have an understanding of where the other stands on the issue, you'll need to make your own decision as to whether or not to go through with the marriage. There are several possible outcomes. You may decide that being with your partner is more important than having children and decide to go forward. You may decide the opposite—you've always wanted children and can't go through with a marriage that won't include them.

If you and your partner agree that you do want children, take time to discuss the following: religion, education, discipline, where to live (what neighborhood and whether or not you'll live close to family), childcare, and whether or not one parent will stay home with the kids, work part-time, or work at home.

Making a list of your goals will help bridge the gap between you and your spouse on child rearing and will assist in creating the brightest future you can for your child. Answering the following questionnaire will also help you both understand what you want for your child (children) without unwanted surprises after your family has expanded.

MAYBE BABY QUESTIONNAIRE

1. Do you want children?

MY RESPONSE _____

_____

_____

YOUR RESPONSE _____

_____

_____

2. At what age would you like to begin our family?

MY RESPONSE _____

_____

YOUR RESPONSE _____

_____

3. How many children do you want to have?

MY RESPONSE _____

_____

YOUR RESPONSE _____

_____

4. Are we financially ready for children?
   How will we pay for our children's college education?

MY RESPONSE _____

_____

_____

YOUR RESPONSE _____

_____

_____

5. Who will care for the children?
   Will one of us be a stay-at-home parent?
   Will we use daycare? Will we have a nanny?

MY RESPONSE _____

_____

_____

YOUR RESPONSE _____

_____

_____

6. Will we raise our children to follow a particular religion?
   If so, what religion?

MY RESPONSE _____

_____

YOUR RESPONSE _____

_____

7. Do you have any other financial obligations regarding child support
   or alimony from prior relationships? If so, how much and what are
   the terms of the prior agreement?

MY RESPONSE _____

_____

_____

YOUR RESPONSE _____

_____

_____

8. Do you think our child/children should be assigned chores?

MY RESPONSE _____

_____

YOUR RESPONSE _____

_____

9. What types of activities should our children be enrolled in?

MY RESPONSE _____

_____

YOUR RESPONSE _____

_____

10. Should they go to public, private, or home school?

MY RESPONSE _____

_____

YOUR RESPONSE _____

_____

11. Who will be the disciplinarian?

MY RESPONSE _____

_____

YOUR RESPONSE _____

_____

Alternate Routes to Parenthood

Whether you are in a heterosexual or same-sex relationship, adoption may be an option for you and your partner. Some couples who are able to conceive a child actually prefer to adopt, either because they like the idea of giving a home to a child who would otherwise not have one or because they don't have time or the energy to try to become pregnant. Some opt for a surrogate. If indeed you want children but don't want to or can't go the traditional route, it's important to discuss alternatives with your spouse. The issue can become loaded when one partner wishes to pursue parenthood at all costs while the other has a limit to how much time or energy he or she is willing to invest in making that dream come true. The stress of not being able to conceive can take a toll on a marriage. The often long process of waiting for an adoption to come through can also lead to tension and uncertainty. Reading through this next section will help you make decisions should you find yourself in the position of looking for an alternative route to parenthood.

ADOPTION

Adopting a child can be one of the most special events in a couple's life. I will never forget the day my family brought home my brother. We accepted him into our family from the second we laid eyes on him and he is one of the most special people in my life. I could not envision my life without him. Some couples may hold extended family meetings to acquire moral support and assistance during the transitional period of adoption. It is a helpful way to get all of your loved ones on board for the special day when you receive your bundle of joy.

If you and your partner feel the urge or need to raise a child and cannot or chose not to have one the traditional way, adopting may be the right choice for you. However, it is no easy feat, and the process, as described by many, is daunting. It is up to you and your partner to dig deep and decide if building a family is right for you. Ask yourselves: Why do we want a child? Do we prefer to try to have a child that is biologically ours or provide a home for a child who doesn't have one?

If you decide to adopt a child, you should discuss certain issues in advance: Will it be an open adoption, in which the birth parents are known and involved in the child's life? Or a closed adoption, in which your child may not ever know who gave him or her up for adoption? These are very serious questions that take a great deal of thought, assistance from professionals, and even counselors to try and create a safe and comfortable environment for your child and family.

Research how adoption or foster care works and attend classes in your area if they are available. There are many different ways to bring an adopted child into your life.

DIFFERENT TYPES OF ADOPTION

DOMESTIC ADOPTION is the adoption of children who reside in the US, either through the public child welfare system or private adoption.

FOSTER CARE ADOPTION is the adoption of a child from state custody when reunification with birth parents is not possible for safety or other reasons. It is arranged by state child welfare agencies or by private agencies under contract with the states. Children may be adopted by their foster parents, relatives (who may or may not have been caring for the child through kinship foster care), or adults to whom they have no prior relationship. Adoption from foster care has increased in the past five years in response to a federal mandate that states take timely action to provide permanent homes for children in state care.

PRIVATE ADOPTION can be arranged either through an agency or through independent adoption. In private agency adoption, children are placed through a nonprofit or for-profit agency that is licensed by the state.

In INDEPENDENT ADOPTION, children are placed directly with adoptive parents by birth parents or with the help of a facilitator or attorney.

INTERNATIONAL ADOPTION is the adoption of children from a country outside of the US. International adoptions are usually arranged through adoption agencies. Adoptions are finalized abroad or in the United States, depending on the laws of the country where the child was born.

TRANSRACIAL ADOPTION refers to children who are placed with an adoptive family of another race or ethnicity. While it is a subgroup of both domestic and international adoption, it is frequently discussed as a separate category due to the unique cultural issues faced by the new families.

GAY ADOPTION is the term used to describe adoption either by a single homosexual person or a same-sex couple. There are a number of ways in which a same-sex couple may go about adopting a child. First, if one of the partners has legal custody over the child from a previous relationship, the new partner may seek to adopt the child. This is called *second-parent adoption*, and allows the parent who currently has custody to retain that right. Another route is *joint adoption*, which happens when the couple is not married, but wants to adopt a child together. *Stepparent adoption* would be the alternative if the couple is in a recognized domestic partnership. If the same-sex couple lives in a state where they are not legally permitted to adopt a child, they may assume *guardianship* over the child, which doesn't carry the same rights as adoption.

Each country, state, and province has its own laws on gay adoption, so it's important to become familiar with the law in the place where you live.

CHILDREN FROM A PRIOR MARRIAGE OR RELATIONSHIP

If you used to be married or had a child from a previous relationship and are getting married, it is crucial for you and your spouse to talk about it. Co-parenting a child who is not biologically yours can be a wonderful experience, but it can also come with a great deal of stress. The "ex" can become an interloper in your marriage, creating tension around issues of money, visitation, pick up and drop off, vacations, work, lifestyle, and a number of other issues. If your partner has a good relationship with his or her ex, call a family meeting to discuss the boundaries and expectations before you wed to ensure everyone is on the same page and has the child's best interest at heart.

Be clear on who is paying for what. If there is a child support payment, what does it cover? Who will be responsible for funding a college account and actually paying for college? Will you require the child to work during the school year or in the summers? Who will pay for vacations? When will you see the child on major holidays and birthdays? These are crucial topics to discuss with your partner BEFORE you get married. If

TIPS FOR SUCCESSFUL STEPPARENTING

Parent as a team

Never badmouth the child's biological parents

Know your role

Support your child

Never use your child as a messenger

Communicate wisely

Maintain consistency for the child

Let your child have a voice

these topics are not addressed and agreed upon, you will surely see some discord in your marriage.

GOING FORWARD AS A "BLENDED" FAMILY

A child must feel unconditionally loved by each stepparent. That's especially true if you and your partner later decide to have a child together. There should be no distinction between any child in the family. This can be difficult at times and may require the help of a counselor who can help the stepparent come to terms with what it means to be in a blended family. However, being a stepparent can also be a wonderful role to play. You can be a friend, a confidant, a supporter, a cheerleader: someone with whom a child can discuss thoughts and feelings in a confidential manner. It can take a long time for such a relationship to develop, but when it does, it can be a true asset to both the child and stepparent.

Living Together

TAKING YOUR (POSSIBLE) MARRIAGE
FOR A TEST DRIVE

The National Institute of Child and Human Development reports "cohabitation, once rare, is now the norm." Recent census data shows that there are 12,000,000 unmarried partners living together in 6,008,007 households (US Census Bureau "American Community Survey: 2005–2007"). In fact, the majority of couples getting married today lived together first (Bumpass, Larry and Lu, HSIEN-HEN 2000 "Trends in Cohabitation and Implications for Children's Family Contacts in the United States" Population Studies, 54:29–41).

Living together before marriage is often considered a trial run for marriage. It allows the prospective spouses to work out the kinks, so to speak, before tying the knot, and that is what premarital planning is all about. Attitudes about living together vary. From a religious perspective, some believe that living together before marriage is morally wrong. Others believe it lacks the binding commitment to support the relationship; if the relationship is not working, either partner can easily move out. Whatever your belief system, it's important for you and your partner to talk about your opinions before you start to think about living together before marriage.

Should you move in with your partner? From a practical perspective, living together can be seen as a way to save money, solidify a relationship, and address concerns that may arise in the future. While it's not quite the same as getting married, moving in with your significant other is a very big step that requires careful thought and consideration. There are many different schools of thought on the issue. Knowing intimate details about your potential spouse is certainly valuable. And it's very difficult to know the ins and outs of a partner's personality and day-to-day habits without really living with him or her. Living with the person you love can be exciting.

But there's another side to the coin. "Living together before marriage may seem like a harmless or even a progressive family trend until one takes a careful look at the evidence," say David Popenoe and Barbara Dafoe Whitehead of the Rutgers University Project. "In fact, living together before marriage seems to have increased the risk of divorcing."

You might remember the 1970s television show *The Odd Couple*. Felix and Oscar, the characters in the series, decided to live together in an apartment in New York City. Felix was the Type A personality who loved everything orderly and in perfect form. Oscar was disorganized, messy, and even downright untidy; a classic Type B. In trying to live together in perfect harmony in a small apartment, the two (who were not romantically involved) experienced many of the common trials and tribulations that come from sharing a space. While it made for great comedy, their conflicts represent exactly what many couples try to avoid when moving in together.

If you decide to live together, it's important to set ground rules. Each of you must understand the other's personality type and personal habits. Does your partner like to do laundry or let it pile up? Does he like to clean, or would it be better to consider hiring a cleaning person to come in on a weekly or biweekly basis? Does one of you like to cook and the other one like to clean? Or do you both dislike cooking and prefer to eat out a lot instead? Who is going to do the food shopping? Who is going to balance the checkbook? Are you even going to use joint accounts or keep your money separate? What side of the bed do you like to sleep on? Do you like to watch TV before you go to sleep or do you like it perfectly quiet? Do you like the window open or do you have allergies that would be negatively affected by air coming in through the bedroom window? Do you like your mattress firm or do you like it soft? How much closet space do you need? One person may have tons of clothes and the other not so much, or both of you may need an equal amount of space. And don't forget that couples also often argue about how to decorate.

Although these habits, traits, and personal tastes may seem unimportant, they can be crucial to determining compatibility between two people who are living together. If you had a roommate in college or had a sibling growing up, you know it can be hard to live with someone whose habits differ from yours. Little things can get under your skin.

If living together before you get married is an option you're considering, take the following quiz to help you think it through.

THE COHABITATION COMPATIBILITY QUIZ

1. What is your current living situation?

MY RESPONSE _____

_____

_____

YOUR RESPONSE _____

_____

_____

2. Do you intend to marry or just live together?

MY RESPONSE _____

_____

_____

YOUR RESPONSE _____

_____

_____

3. Why would your partner be interested in moving in with you?

MY RESPONSE _____

_____

YOUR RESPONSE _____

_____

4. Have you discussed and planned out your finances?

MY RESPONSE _____

_____

YOUR RESPONSE _____

_____

5. What are your motivations for moving in together?
   Do you see these as the right reasons?

MY RESPONSE _____

_____

YOUR RESPONSE _____

_____

6. Is moving in together more about convenience than about bringing
   your relationship to the next level?

MY RESPONSE _____

_____

YOUR RESPONSE _____

_____

7. What habits have you seen from your partner that you would like him or her to improve upon before you move in together?

MY RESPONSE _____

_____

YOUR RESPONSE _____

_____

8. Are you ready to share your personal space with the person you love on a day-to-day basis?

MY RESPONSE _____

_____

YOUR RESPONSE _____

_____

9. Do you feel excited to move in with your partner?

MY RESPONSE _____

_____

YOUR RESPONSE _____

_____

10. Are you mature enough to cope with the pressure of living with another person at this point in your life?

MY RESPONSE _____

_____

YOUR RESPONSE _____

_____

COHABITATION AGREEMENTS

When you get married, marital laws apply from the date the civil ceremony takes place. At that time, you and your partner can argue that you have a right to receive certain property and or support based upon the income acquired during the marriage. Spouses automatically receive survivor benefits from retirement plans, potentially receive social security and insurance benefits, and inherit assets acquired during the marriage, unless there is a prenuptial agreement in place (see page 121).

Unmarried couples do not legally have those rights unless they expressly secure them in a cohabitation agreement. This private contract between two cohabitants sets out the rights and obligations as if the two parties were married without marital law specifically applying. If you decide to move in together and don't set a specific wedding date, you may choose to create a cohabitation agreement, which will determine rights and responsibilities, distribution of assets, and even inheritance and insurance

COMMON LAW MARRIAGE

Common law marriage, also called *sui juris marriage,* is an "informal" marriage that is established by habit of living together over a period of time without having completed a recognized form of marriage ceremony. It is recognized legally in some jurisdictions (and carries rights in those places), but not in others. In some parts of Europe, for example, common law marriage is the term used to describe domestic partnerships. In general, the term common law marriage describes a domestic partnership in which both parties are over the age of 18, consent to live with each other, and are not legally married to someone else.

Common law marriages are recognized in the following US states: Alabama, Colorado, Iowa, Kansas, Arkansas, Montana, New Mexico, Rhode Island, South Carolina, Texas, Utah, and the District of Columbia. In New Hampshire, common law marriage can be recognized posthumously, which means that any couple who lived together for three years and "acknowledge each other as husband and wife" can inherit from one another.

COHABITATION AGREEMENT CHECKLIST

As you plan your cohabitation agreement, consider the following questions.

1. If you have medical concerns, would you like to give your partner power for medical directives?

2. Would like to keep your partner as a beneficiary in some or all of your estate?

3. Would like to have defined financial responsibilities for the household?

4. Who will pay debts on a monthly basis?

5. If you purchase property together, how you will you share the tax obligation and deduction?

6. How you will distribute shared property in the event of your untimely death before you ever marry?

For the purpose of further discussion between you and your partner, I have included a sample cohabitation agreement (page 171).

issues. Each party signs the agreement with the assistance of separate legal counsel. As long as the cohabitation agreement is fair and counsel has been sought, judges in most states will generally enforce a fair and equitable cohabitation agreement in the event of a legal dispute by one party or the other. Cohabitation agreements have been more popular in same-sex relationships before entering civil unions and same-sex marriages.

It's important to determine whether or not a cohabitation agreement is right for you by seeking an attorney in your state who is licensed in family law. While the sample agreement (page 171) provides you with guidance about cohabitation agreements, it by no means gives you advice about executing a cohabitation agreement. If you decide to do so, seek expert counsel to get the pros and cons of actually entering into an agreement.

A cohabitation agreement can be viewed just like a prenuptial agreement in that it allows a couple to determine who will keep specific assets that come into the relationship and determines what will happen in the event of separation. The real difference is that a cohabitation agreement is triggered when a couple moves in together, while a prenuptial agreement goes into effect after a couple marries. If you're thinking about a cohabitation agreement, start by declaring the property each of you owned prior to entering the relationship. All of these assets need to be listed in the cohabitation agreement and may include (but not be limited to) vehicles, bank accounts, pension funds, retirement accounts, homes, and specific property other than real estate, including furniture, heirlooms, art, and other items of value. All of the assets listed should include a general value as well as a bank statement or appraisal of the item if it's available.

It's also important to list all of your liabilities. Count values at the time you intend to move in together. Determine who will pay for which living expenses and how those expenses will be paid each month. You should also decide what will happen to property acquired jointly during your cohabitation period. If you enter into a cohabitation agreement and later decide to get married, you can either terminate the agreement or convert the terms into a prenuptial agreement, which will be binding after you actually get married and have your civil ceremony.

Second Time Around

REMARRIAGE

"The arithmetic of love is unique:
two halves do not make a whole,
only two wholes make a half."
—Jo Coudert

So, it's your second or third time walking down aisle. You're smarter and wiser about what it takes to be in happy marriage, right? You saw what went wrong in your prior relationship and want to make this marriage last. But you may be surprised to learn that the rate of break-ups for second and third marriages *increases*, rather than decreases over time. "Why?" you may ask. My personal opinion is that, in general, people don't learn from their mistakes and are unable to change behaviors. Instead, it's the rebound syndrome or cycle. It is, at times, too painful to look in the mirror and take inventory, openly and honestly. Your remarriage is an opportunity to do so. It's up to you to stop the cycle of bad relationships now.

In many ways, I think people who remarry have a huge advantage over those who have never been married. You know what to expect and what works and what doesn't. Implementing the strategies and techniques outlined in this book will be a vital tool for strengthening your marital skills the second or third time around. You can acknowledge and work on the challenges that arose in your past relationship and make sure that you modify your present behavior based on what you've learned. As Dr. Phil (who has been married for 33 years) says, "Falling in love is not the same thing as being in love. Embrace the change and know it takes work."

What about the kids? The issue of children from prior marriages can sometimes cause conflict in a second marriage. It's crucial to set boundaries and establish points of reference from the outset to determine how you will relate to each other's children. This should include the financial ramifications of their inheritances, any costs associated with their education or upbringing, and, for some couples, the consideration of grandchildren. Talking about these ever-so-important topics can make or break a marriage. It's very difficult for blended families to coexist without conflict. Understanding the temperament of each side of the family and where your boundaries lie will be extremely helpful when preparing to wed.

Here are some helpful tips for approaching topics that must be addressed with your partner before you remarry:

- Hold a meeting with both sides of the family to go over ground rules for their roles and expectations in your marriage.
- Talk to your partner about money and how you will coexist financially.
- Discuss the need to create wills. How would you like to leave your assets, and to whom?
- Talk openly about the possibility of entering into a prenuptial agreement.
- Listen to one another about your concerns for the future.

Agree to work with professionals to help sort out any family, insurance, or inheritance issues peacefully. Use the tips and tools in this book to break the old habits you had from childhood so you can enter

REMARRIAGE STATISTICS compiled from the
National Center for Health Statistics (2002) show:

- 54 percent of divorced women remarry within five years
- 75 percent of divorced women remarry within ten years
- Black women are the least likely to remarry
- White women are the most likely to remarry

into your new marriage with a fresh perspective. Make this newfound approach to your marriage a fun journey. Use the questionnaires as exercises to get to know each other better. Decide on a night to go over a few chapters, then arrange for dinner and dancing to reward your hard work. Creating fun and exciting ways to maintain a strong marriage will be part of your success. Play by your rules no one else's. Only you and your partner know what works for both of you.

SECOND TIME AROUND QUIZ

1. Why are you marrying your partner?

MY RESPONSE _____

_____

_____

YOUR RESPONSE _____

_____

_____

2. Are you confident this marriage makes sense? Why?

MY RESPONSE _____

_____

_____

YOUR RESPONSE _____

_____

_____

3. What do you love about your partner?

MY RESPONSE _____

_____

_____

YOUR RESPONSE _____

_____

_____

4. Why will this marriage be different?

MY RESPONSE _____

_____

_____

YOUR RESPONSE _____

_____

_____

5. What will you do differently in this marriage?

MY RESPONSE _____

_____

_____

YOUR RESPONSE _____

_____

_____

Ready or Not?

You may be satisfied that your current relationship is strong. But becoming a spouse is very different than being a boyfriend or girlfriend. The role of a spouse is much more serious and comes with huge responsibilities. Marriage should be a forever proposition: two people form a union for eternity—not until one decides to find a guy with more hair or a younger, more voluptuous woman. Take this Premarital Quiz to make sure you are both ready when you say your I do's.

THE MARRIAGE READINESS QUIZ

1. Would *you* marry you?

MY RESPONSE   YES_____   NO_____

_____

YOUR RESPONSE   YES_____   NO_____

_____

2. Do you want a marriage like your parents' marriage? Why or why not?

MY RESPONSE   YES_____   NO_____

_____

YOUR RESPONSE   YES_____   NO_____

_____

3. Are you and your partner best friends?

MY RESPONSE   YES_____   NO_____

_____

YOUR RESPONSE   YES_____   NO_____

_____

4. If you were stranded on a remote island, would your partner be your perfect companion?

MY RESPONSE   YES_____   NO_____

_____

YOUR RESPONSE   YES_____   NO_____

_____

5. Do you keep big secrets from your partner?

MY RESPONSE   YES_____   NO_____

_____

YOUR RESPONSE   YES_____   NO_____

_____

6. Does your partner know your biggest flaws?
   If so, does your partner accept you despite them?

MY RESPONSE   YES_____   NO_____

_____

_____

YOUR RESPONSE   YES_____   NO_____

_____

_____

7. After an argument, can you kiss and make up or do you hold a grudge?

MY RESPONSE·   YES_____   NO_____

YOUR RESPONSE   YES_____   NO_____

8. Can you name your partner's three best friends?

MY RESPONSE   YES_____   NO_____

LIST_____

YOUR RESPONSE   YES_____   NO_____

LIST_____

9. Do you know what stresses your partner is currently facing?

MY RESPONSE   YES_____   NO_____

YOUR RESPONSE   YES_____   NO_____

10. Do you know some of you partner's life dreams?

MY RESPONSE   YES_____   NO_____

YOUR RESPONSE   YES_____   NO_____

11. Do you know your partner's basic philosophy of life?

MY RESPONSE   YES_____   NO_____

_____

YOUR RESPONSE   YES_____   NO_____

_____

12. Do you feel that your partner knows you well?

MY RESPONSE   YES_____   NO_____

_____

YOUR RESPONSE   YES_____   NO_____

_____

13. Do you share the same basic view and philosophies on life?

MY RESPONSE   YES_____   NO_____

_____

YOUR RESPONSE   YES_____   NO_____

_____

14. Do you love your partner unconditionally?

MY RESPONSE   YES_____   NO_____

_____

YOUR RESPONSE   YES_____   NO_____

_____

15. Do you love your partner's quirks?

MY RESPONSE   YES_____   NO_____

_____

YOUR RESPONSE　　　　YES_____　　　NO_____

16. Do you know that your partner is not perfect, and will you accept that he or she may not change?

MY RESPONSE　　　　YES_____　　　NO_____

YOUR RESPONSE　　　　YES_____　　　NO_____

17. Do you love being home with your partner watching TV or reading a great book?

MY RESPONSE　　　　YES_____　　　NO_____

YOUR RESPONSE　　　　YES_____　　　NO_____

18. Will you be able to handle not going out with your friends every night?

MY RESPONSE　　　　YES_____　　　NO_____

YOUR RESPONSE　　　　YES_____　　　NO_____

If you answered most of the 18 questions with a yes, you have a strong foundation for a marriage. If not, think about whether or not you're really ready to take your relationship to that next step.

THE TOUGH QUESTIONS

The following questions are designed to make you think about your mate and whether or not you're ready to get married.

Take time alone to answer these questions honestly. Don't lie to yourself—it will only produce false results, and, ultimately, disappointment in your marriage.

1. Are you afraid of being alone and single?

   MY RESPONSE   YES_____   NO_____

   YOUR RESPONSE   YES_____   NO_____

2. Do you want to be cared for by someone without putting in the appropriate work to care for him or her as well?

   MY RESPONSE   YES_____   NO_____

   YOUR RESPONSE   YES_____   NO_____

3. Do you feel the need to get married because all of your friends are tying the knot?

   MY RESPONSE   YES_____   NO_____

   YOUR RESPONSE   YES_____   NO_____

4. Are you fully committed to your partner?

   MY RESPONSE   YES_____   NO_____

   YOUR RESPONSE   YES_____   NO_____

5. Do you love your partner (but are not necessarily in love with him or her)?

   MY RESPONSE   YES_____   NO_____

   YOUR RESPONSE   YES_____   NO_____

6. Are you best friends but not lovers?

   MY RESPONSE   YES_____   NO_____

   YOUR RESPONSE   YES_____   NO_____

7. Are you really only looking to be rescued from your life and current living arrangements?

MY RESPONSE   YES_____   NO_____

YOUR RESPONSE   YES_____   NO_____

8. Are you aware of any red flags in your relationship or in your partner, but are willing to overlook them in order to wed?

MY RESPONSE   YES_____   NO_____

_____

_____

_____

_____

YOUR RESPONSE   YES_____   NO_____

_____

_____

_____

_____

FINAL COMMITMENT QUIZ

Answer the following questions:

1. I have and will continue to be monogamous sexually and emotionally with my partner.

MY RESPONSE   YES_____   NO_____

YOUR RESPONSE   YES_____   NO_____

2. I am ready to merge my life with my partner and not live as a single person any longer.

MY RESPONSE   YES_____   NO_____

YOUR RESPONSE   YES_____   NO_____

3. I have resolved most of my past relationship concerns and have a clear head moving forward with my partner.

MY RESPONSE   YES_____   NO_____

YOUR RESPONSE   YES_____   NO_____

4. I understand what it means to commit and to make my partner number one.

MY RESPONSE   YES_____   NO_____

YOUR RESPONSE   YES_____   NO_____

5. I am able to keep my work separate and not allow it to interfere in my relationship.

MY RESPONSE   YES_____   NO_____

YOUR RESPONSE   YES_____   NO_____

6. I understand the meaning of love and am unconditionally committed to and in love with my partner.

MY RESPONSE   YES_____   NO_____

YOUR RESPONSE   YES_____   NO_____

If you can answer all of these questions in the affirmative, you are ready to take the plunge and marry the person of your dreams.

Making It LEGAL

The letter of the law behind your wedding and marriage

Legally Wed

Now that you've decided that you're really ready to get married, it's time to start thinking about what that means in the eyes of the law. First, you'll need to know how to acquire your marriage license before your ceremony. Every state requires a marriage license to legalize your marriage; you can't get married without it. But it doesn't matter *where* you actually get married. Even if you get married outside of the US, every state must recognize a valid marriage under the Full Faith and Credit Clause of the US Constitution, Article IV, which "requires states to recognize and enforce the legislative acts, public records, and judicial decisions of other states."

What is a marriage license? It's a document issued by a public authority that grants a couple permission to legally get married. It's your responsibility to file for it and acquire it in advance of your ceremony. Both you and your partner must sign the marriage license application in person at the county clerk's office or local municipality (depending on where you reside). Every state has its own unique laws, so researching in advance will help you navigate the process.

Here are some important factors to consider when applying for your marriage license:

- Bring proof of identity to the clerk's office. That might mean your driver's license, passport, or social security card, as well as proof of your address, such as a piece of mail.

- Ask for a few copies of your marriage license (it may cost extra) because you might need them. Try for a certified copy. When you decide to change your name, you need an original to show the motor vehicle bureau, credit unions, payroll departments, and other state or federal agencies.

❥ If you were previously married, be sure to provide the clerk written proof of your prior judgment of divorce, annulment, dissolution, or proof of a prior marriage that resulted in death.

❥ Many states have eliminated the blood test requirement, but be sure to contact your county clerk or the marriage license center in your municipality to get the most updated information available.

CIVIL VS. RELIGIOUS CEREMONIES

In the early planning process, you and your partner should decide what type of ceremony you prefer: civil or religious. This decision is really up to the two of you and should be discussed and re-solved, especially if there are religious differences or family requests for cultural ceremonies. You may want to discuss your options with a civil official or your rabbi, minister, or priest to determine what the advantages and disadvantages are for both types of ceremonies.

A civil ceremony is performed by a legal official and can take place in a courtroom at your local courthouse. Or you can opt for a ceremony in any other location except a religious house of worship as long as the officiant is properly recognized to marry you. Most people who are not religious, cannot agree on religion, or have no affinity for organized religion usually only have a civil ceremony. On the other hand, a religious ceremony usually entails one type of faith, although two can be merged if you and your partner wish.

Most religious ceremonies have a style or format chosen by the clergy officiating the ceremony, as well as traditions that must be followed. Talk to your rabbi, minister, or priest to understand exactly what will occur during the ceremony and what you can do to modify certain parts that you may not be comfortable following. Regardless, the type of ceremony you have will depend on what makes the most sense for you and your partner. Try not to be influenced by others as the decision should feel right to you.

Individual states have their own specific requirements. At least 20 states require couples to wait several days from the time the marriage license is issued to the time the ceremony is performed. The theory is that you need to be sure you are ready to wed. The waiting period is designed to eliminate last minute cases of cold feet. Here are a few of the states' waiting requirements:

ONE-DAY WAITING PERIOD: New York, Illinois, South Carolina, Delaware

THREE-DAY WAITING PERIOD: New Jersey, Oregon, Kansas, Washington, Maine, Massachusetts, Mississippi, Michigan

FIVE-DAY WAITING PERIOD: District of Columbia, Minnesota

You must be at least 18 years of age to legally marry. If you're younger, you must have the written consent of a parent in most states. Only a few states require proof of vaccinations. Double-check on this issue at your local clerk's office to make sure.

What is a marriage ceremony? It is the religious or civil preceding that solemnizes a marriage. It must be performed by someone who is recognized with the authority to do so (some examples would be a judge, justice of the peace, certified officiant, or a religious official). The marriage must be witnessed by someone who can attest that the officiant is qualified to perform the ceremony.

After the ceremony is performed, the officiant must provide proof that the ceremony took place—this is called the marriage *certificate*. This document is filed with the state agency that records marriage certificates. This is a crucial step in solidifying your marriage. I would suggest following up 30 days after your wedding ceremony and honeymoon to be sure your marriage certificate was filed and received in accordance with the state guidelines.

Name Changes

To change your name or not? It's a big question for many. Some women add their married name to the end of their names and some hyphenate. Some keep their maiden names. What is your preference? How does your significant other feel about taking his or her last name? Or not? Once you have spoken and agreed on a name change, here is how you go about accomplishing this procedural task.

STEPS TO TAKE TO LEGALLY CHANGE YOUR NAME

1. Obtain a certified copy of your marriage license from the agency that filed and registered your license.

2. Visit the Social Security Administration office near you to amend your name and ID for payroll withholdings and retirement benefits, when applicable. If you don't do this, the IRS may reject your tax return filing, so make sure this is done efficiently and properly. You may need to file specific forms to obtain a new social security card as well. Ask questions to be sure you are completing the process correctly the first time.

3. Obtain a new driver's license at the Department of Motor Vehicles using the appropriate proof of your residency. Go to the DMV website to determine what documents you need to bring with you as each department has different requirements.

4. Notify your bank, insurance agency (homeowner's), medical administrator, and credit union to change your name and update your records on file for future mailings.

5. Notify credit card companies, landlord, doctor, passport office, professional licensing boards, voter registry, and other professional organizations of your name change.

6. Update your employer's records for payroll and benefits.

Remember: getting a marriage license with your married name does not automatically change your name legally. Take the steps above to make sure you legally change your name and enjoy your new persona!

TO BE MY WEDDED SPOUSE

Take a look at some of the traditional vows that you may or may not say to your spouse on your special day. Read them out loud, read them to your partner, and consider how you will be committed to your vows in the future. Will you "have this woman to be thy wedded wife to live together in holy matrimony?" Will you "love, comfort and honor her in sickness and in health for as long as you both shall live?" Will you "have this man, to wed, to obey him, serve him, love him, honor him and keep him in sickness and in health as long as you shall live?"

Make two or three versions of vows you would like to say during your ceremony. They should be special and come from the heart. Then have your partner write his or hers. Compare your results and find out if you are on the same track.

MY VOWS _____

_____

_____

_____

_____

YOUR VOWS _____

_____

_____

_____

_____

_____

Making or Updating a Will

Many people mistakenly believe that a will is for the elderly. That is not the case. I have seen many young people pass away unexpectedly, leaving their significant others and young children unprotected due to the lack of proper estate planning. When you're planning on spending your life with someone, it's time to discuss the need for a will. If you have one already in place, bravo. But just be cognizant of the fact that it must be updated after you wed and/or have a child.

Some may ask "Why is a will important if I feel healthy and my parents are still alive and in their 90s?" First and foremost, no one can predict the future. Why not prepare for an unforeseen circumstance rather than leave the division of your estate to the state? Or worse, if you and your spouse pass away simultaneously in a car accident, for example, who will care for your child? What will happen to the accumulated wealth you worked so hard to obtain? Creating a concept for your will ensures that the people you love most will inherit your property and even your ability to designate funds to your favorite charity. Your will is also a place to identify people for specific roles such as guardian for minor children, trustees who will manage your property, and executor for your estate.

Once you have determined that a will is necessary, discuss your separate and combined desires with your partner, including the possibility that you both may die together. Although these are very tough topics, they are crucial to premarital planning. Trust me. When lightning strikes, you don't want to be pressured into making important decisions under emotional duress.

Thinking about who to designate your property to, setting up a college fund via a trust for your children, and thinking about a guardian for your children are all necessary preplanning topics that are critical to resolve in the early stages of a union. Finalizing your will can set your mind at ease about the what if's, and will guarantee your instructions be known and followed after your passing. Without a will, state laws apply and can get very complicated, especially if you both pass away simultaneously or one of you files for divorce before the other's passing.

The Fun Side of Wedding Planning

There are so many websites and tools that you can use to start the planning stages of your wedding. I have consolidated a plan to suggest the topics to discuss and focus on with your partner. When I was planning my wedding, I did a great deal of research online, gathering information from www.theknot.com and www.weddingwire.com. I then created a filing system and began labeling folders for each topic that I needed to address and handle in an orderly fashion. Here are some tips to determine what you will need to do within a 12-month window after you become engaged!

9 TO 12 MONTHS IN ADVANCE

You're engaged. Hooray!

Start a wedding binder. Create file folders labeling them clearly with topics such as reception, caterer, florist, musician, hairstylist, budget, etc.

Start looking through bridal magazines to get a flavor for wedding dresses, tuxedos, etc.

Start thinking about how many people you and your partner want to invite to the wedding (dependent on budget).

Discuss who will pay for what and if you will get contributions from family members.

Start thinking of a wedding theme, location, and venue—will it be a small venue, destination wedding, or outside wedding in a garden?

Hire a wedding planner if affordable and necessary.

Start thinking about who will be in your bridal party. If you have more than a best man and maid of honor, match up an even number of people so each person walking down the aisle has a partner.

10 MONTHS IN ADVANCE

Research photographers, bands, ceremony musicians, videographers, DJs, florists, and officiants (civil or religious ceremony).

Begin to look for wedding gowns and a honeymoon destination.

Create a bridal registry for your wedding gifts and/or engagement party, if applicable.

8 TO 9 MONTHS IN ADVANCE

Have an engagement party, if desired.

Hire all vendors: reserve dates and have signed contracts.

Choose and meet with your caterer.

Buy your dress.

Reserve hotel rooms for out-of-town guests (usually blocks of rooms on the same floor).

Think about reserving a website and posting updates for your friends and family.

7 TO 8 MONTHS IN ADVANCE

Select and purchase invitations and hire a calligrapher or determine to do it yourself.

Send save-the-date cards.

Finalize the guest list.

Shop for bridesmaids' dresses.

Shop for groom, groomsmen, and fathers'/stepfathers' outfits.

Discuss mothers'/stepmothers' attire.

Meet with officiant to discuss time of service and details.

Book a rehearsal dinner location.

5 TO 7 MONTHS IN ADVANCE

Order the cake, if it's not already included in the caterer's contract.

3 TO 6 MONTHS IN ADVANCE

Send guest list to the host of your shower, if applicable.

Schedule hair and makeup practice, and then finalize actual time for the day of the wedding.

Decide if the bridal party will be utilizing stylists and who will be paying.

Choose your music list, including special dances and intermission music.

Finalize your menu (tasting, if still necessary) and flower order.

Order favors.

Make a list of people who will speak at the wedding and any other special events.

Purchase your special lingerie/decide what jewelry you will wear (garter, something borrowed, etc.).

Print programs or menus.

Purchase wedding bands.

2 TO 3 MONTHS IN ADVANCE

Start addressing thank you's once you have printed your final guest list.

Make honeymoon arrangements.

Confirm rehearsal dinner.

Confirm and contact all vendors to make sure all dates are in their master book.

Meet with photographer and videographer.

Enjoy the bachelor and bachelorette parties!

Arrange to apply for a marriage license (get blood test if required).

Schedule the fittings for the bride and attendants. Don't forget shoes and accessories.

1 MONTH IN ADVANCE

Buy gifts for the bridal party.

Send final payment to most vendors.

Confirm limo driver knows locations and directions.

Create seating chart.

Write vows if applicable.

Buy wedding props: pillow for ring, guestbook sign in, candles, etc.

Buy gift for your partner, if applicable.

Double-check hotel reservations for out-of-town guests.

WEEKS LEADING UP TO THE WEDDING: COUNTDOWN

Send final guest list and seating chart to caterer.

Send in post office change of address, if applicable.

Place ad in periodical about your nuptials.

Confirm receipt of your marriage license.

Confirm rings, shoes, and accessories for the special day.

Assemble welcome baskets for hotel guests.

Try on wedding gown and tuxedo.

Book a relaxing treatment.

Put all vendor money aside, plus set aside gratuities for each vendor at the wedding.

Talk to attendants and bridal party to make sure they know the time to arrive for pictures and their places at ceremony.

1 TO 2 DAYS IN ADVANCE

Enjoy the rehearsal dinner or lunch.

Get a manicure and pedicure.

Males: get an old-fashioned shave and massage.

Review all contracts.

Eat a small meal.

Hydrate! Breathe! Meditate!

Vendor Contracts

Although planning your wedding can often seem as if it's a fairytale, negotiating vendor contracts can be a bit more daunting. As an attorney, I view these contracts quite seriously, and so should you. These vendors are there to work for you and carry out your vision on your wedding day. But you're not the only one on their minds. Several weddings can take place on any given day, which means your wedding may be compromised. Moreover, while you're celebrating your wedding you won't be in the state of mind to check to see if everything you paid for is in perfect order. That's why it's important to have a family member accompany you to the vendor meetings, read through all the contracts, and be at the reception early to ensure your wedding day is perfect and right!

Vendor contracts are binding legal documents that must be reviewed very carefully. If you can have an attorney peruse them before you sign them, great. If not, make sure you understand every line before you execute. Even one word can make a difference. For example, what if you have a parent with a chronic illness? If he or she was unable to attend your wedding, you want the right to postpone the wedding. Language must be clear in the contract to state your intention. If it isn't, and you had to postpone your wedding, you would likely lose your deposit, unnecessarily. I always suggest adding clauses about illness or unforeseen accidents that will allow you to adjourn the wedding and retain your deposit.

Next, be clear about every word. If you don't understand any language contained in the agreement ASK! Don't be afraid. No question is too silly. This is your big day and you have a great deal of time and money riding on the wedding being spectacular. Once you and the vendor sign the contract, little can be done to modify it in advance of the wedding.

WEDDING VENDOR TIPS

❯ Try to pay with a credit card so that if there is a cancellation or a dispute, you can fight the credit card company and have a better chance of receiving a refund. You can also gain miles on the right credit card and maybe apply them to your honeymoon.

❯ Don't be afraid to ask for references. This is your special day and you want it to be handled professionally.

❯ Do your homework about vendors. Once you choose them, you are locked in. If something goes wrong, and you're not protected, you will likely lose your deposit. Use reputable vendors and you will likely have a smooth wedding without disruption.

Know the terms of the contracts. Make sure each contract has the correct wedding date, time, expectations of the vendor, and costs. Be specific and detailed. If you have a contract with a florist, specify how many bouquets, type of flowers, number of centerpieces, accessories, added fees for delivery time, and other costs. Ask about the cost of bouquets and boutonnieres, decorations, aisle runners, etc.

If you have a contract with a caterer, you want to be clear on cost per plate, type of meal (buffet or seated service), style and size of glassware, plates, type of cutlery, seat covers, linens, and whether or not the wedding cake is included in the total. Ask how many servers will be available and their ratio to the number of tables. Get a seating chart of the location to arrange your tables. Discuss what liquor will be served with dinner and how the bar service and fees work. Also, ask about taxes and whether gratuities are included in your total price.

Likewise, the photographer's contract has similar components. You must specify in the contract how many pictures will be included in your package, cost of a video (unless you hire a separate videographer), and how many albums you will be getting. Some experts recommend not paying the photographer in full until you receive your albums after the wedding. Try to put a time limit on the exchange, such as 30 to 45 days, so you can keep track of, and keep the pressure on, the photographer to get your albums to you. I've heard too many horror stories about photographers never finishing the albums and newlyweds never receiving the albums they paid for and anticipated.

When it comes to the band or disc jockey for the reception, you should be clear on the total cost and their arrival and departure time, what songs you will have played, and the song for your first dance. Usually you give the musicians a 50 percent deposit upon signing the contract and the remaining balance at the wedding. This ensures that the musicians arrive on time and no substitutes come in their place. Find out how long they will play before they take a break, what music will play while the musicians are on break, and decide if you will offer them a meal or not. If anyone will make a speech at the reception, give the band the names in advance, so they can announce the special people in your wedding party and family.

Similar contracts will likely be executed for hairstylists and make-up artists, limousine and car companies, hotels for guests to stay over, dressmakers, and tuxedo rental. In all of these cases, be sure to read every word of the contract. Make a copy for your records after any contract has been fully executed, and make a clearly marked file to place them in just in case you must reference any of them at any time.

WEDDING VENDOR CONTRACT SAMPLE

The Agreement is made on _____ day of _____ between _____ (you and your partner's name) and (wedding planner/caterer etc.) _____ of _____ tel number _____. _____ (caterer/planner etc.) agrees to the following services to _____ on the _____ date which is their intended wedding date.

1. The services shall include:
   Description of Services
   Flowers
   Rentals
   Music
   Food
   Alcohol/type
   Catering
   Photography
   Lodging
   Ceremony
   Etc.

2. Compensation: The wedding couple or their agent, agrees to pay an initial nonrefundable retainer in the amount of $_____ at the time of signing this agreement. The remaining balance shall be paid as follows: 50 percent due 5 months in advance of the wedding and the entire balance due 10 days in advance of the wedding.

3. Date changes/cancellation: In the event the wedding couple is forced to change or cancel their wedding for the date set above, the provider will try to accommodate a new date. If the wedding is cancelled indefinitely, this provider shall keep the nonrefundable retainer. There may be additional charges incurred for cancellation that may impact the staff and quality of the future event, which the wedding couple shall be responsible to pay for in full.

4. Amendments: This Agreement may be modified or amended if the amendment is made in writing and is signed by all parties heretofore.

5. Accommodations: the patrons hereby agree to conform to all rules and regulations of the premises as well as city, state and federal laws and regulations.

6. Applicable Law: This Agreement shall be governed by the laws of the State of _____ (enter your state).

Before You Sign the Contract

Ask your wedding vendor:

1. How many other weddings will you be serving on our wedding date?

2. How many servers per table?

3. Can you provide two references to ask about their wedding at your establishment?

4. What if there is severe weather? Will you cancel my wedding?

5. Will you be present at my wedding? If there is a problem, who can I talk to during my event?

6. Are there any other fees, taxes, or tips?

7. What if I must postpone the wedding in the event of death of a family member?

Prenuptial Planning

**"An ounce of prevention
is better than a pound of cure."
—Benjamin Franklin**

A prenuptial agreement is a written agreement created and executed by two people before they are legally married. The prenup, as some call it, usually spells out how assets will be distributed in the event of divorce or death. It can also dictate what will happen to property if either party should pass away. It protects each spouse in the event of the other's death, allocates financial responsibility during the marriage, and spells out how a specific dispute would be resolved; for example, whether to go through mediation or arbitration first before going through an expensive litigation.

Contrary to popular opinion, prenups are not just for the rich. Prenuptial agreements have been in existence for thousands of years, dating back to the ancient Egyptians and including European royal families. In the past, parents of the bride and groom were the ones who actually negotiated a type of prenuptial agreement on the couple's behalf. Thank goodness engaged couples today do their own negotiating without their families having full control over their financial and emotional lives.

I believe it is valuable for people to consider entering into a prenuptial agreement if any of the following descriptions apply to you and/or your spouse-to-be:

You own a business

You own real estate

You have received or may receive in the future an inheritance or gift

You earn much more than your partner

Your net worth is much higher than your partner's

You have children from a previous relationship

You have elderly parents that depend on you for financial support

One partner has accumulated a great deal of debt before the marriage

You want to leave your assets to others and not only your partner.

If any of those circumstances describe you, consider a consultation with a highly accredited family law attorney in your state to learn if pursuing a prenuptial agreement would be in your best interest. Take the prenup quiz and share your thoughts with your partner to decide whether or not you collectively believe it's a good idea to secure your assets separately and jointly for the future.

PRENUP QUIZ

Do you have more than $10,000 in credit card debt?   YES_____   NO_____

Do you own real estate?   YES_____   NO_____

Will part or all of your estate go to someone other than your spouse?   YES_____   NO_____

Do you plan on advancing your degree while your partner works before or during the marriage?   YES_____   NO_____

Do you have significant retirement monies?   YES_____   NO_____

Do you earn more than $100,000 per year?   YES_____   NO_____

Do you have a child from a prior
marriage and/or support and
college tuition obligations?   YES_____   NO_____

Do you earn from a business you
own? With or without partners?   YES_____   NO_____

Do you anticipate receiving a large
inheritance?   YES_____   NO_____

When you're considering entering into a prenuptial agreement, ask yourself some important questions and think through your options. What would happen if the two of you decide to divorce and one person suddenly passes away? Will your prenuptial agreement leave one of you struggling and the other, or his/her heirs, well off? Think about balancing and fairly structuring an agreement that would protect your interests. Think about your goals when entering into the prenuptial agreement. Consider your future needs.

Will you have the ability to support yourself in the event of divorce or death of your spouse? What will your contribution be to the education and/or increased earning power of the other? What responsibilities/obligations do you have in your family relationships outside your marriage? Consider the amount of property you own, including real estate and liquid assets.

PRENUPS STATISTICS According to a 2011 report by the American Academy of Matrimonial Lawyers on prenuptial agreements, more women and more middle-class couples are entering into prenuptial agreements than ever before. Part of that increase may be due to the fact that more women are in the workforce and are making more money than ever before. Women have more assets than they ever did and need to plan to avoid conflict should the marriage end in divorce.

Prenuptial agreements are often used as financial planning tools that help resolve many issues regarding property ownership, resolution of debt, division of business interests, spousal support, and other asset-based issues that might arise in the event of a divorce. Good communication about money is essential to ensuring a successful partnership well into the future. But make no mistake about it; bringing up the topic of prenuptial agreements can be extremely difficult, and even starting that financial conversation can be overwhelming.

In my experiences as an attorney and as a professor at Fordham Law School, I've come to believe that negotiating prenuptial agreements opens the lines of financial communication between parties in a marriage whether they like it or not. Marriage is a financial and emotional partnership. A married couple must work together to understand how they will run their financial lives—how they will save, how they will pay down debt, and how they will plan for their financial future and retirement. If a prenuptial agreement is right for you, it should reflect the spirit of your partnership and be viewed as a financial counterpart to your wedding vows.

It is very important to be sensitive to your partner's needs, regardless of whether it was you or your partner who initially wanted the prenuptial agreement. Be careful and considerate in the way you discuss the open issues at hand. I've seen many engagements fall apart and ultimately break up during these negotiations, and I don't want that happening to you. If the terms don't seem equitable or fair, it's important to continue to negotiate until you reach an amicable resolution. Remember, if your future spouse is being unfair or completely one-sided, that's an indication of what your marriage will be. Reasonable people who want to resolve matters fairly can come to an agreement.

If you're thinking about asking your spouse-to-be to enter into a prenuptial agreement, or you know your partner will be asking you to enter into one, you have to be prepared to follow a few procedures in order to create a binding, fair prenuptial agreement. Both parties should have lawyers, which is a requirement in most states. Each lawyer should explain the terms of the agreement to the two of you, and each of you should be clear and articulate about how you want to handle the prenuptial agreement and its negotiations. You and your spouse-to-be need enough time to participate in the negotiations and understand the terms of the agreement. You should seek counsel at least six months prior to the wedding date in order to educate yourself about the laws in your state before you even begin the drafting and negotiating process.

Most states require completion of an accurate, full, and fair disclosure and exchange of all income, assets, and liabilities before the execution of the agreement. As it relates to prenuptial agreements, fair means that the document and procedure are not biased and that one party is not unduly burdened, coerced, or forced into entering into the agreement. In some states, a court may find a prenuptial agreement unfair or invalid (in part or in full) because it was signed last minute (i.e. the day of the wedding or immediately before). Sometimes a judge may strike one part of a prenuptial agreement as unreasonable, but keep the rest of the agreement as enforceable. It's important that you understand the laws of the state where you intend to reside and ask your lawyer all the questions that you deem necessary as you proceed through this important negotiation.

If you decide not to enter into a prenuptial agreement, the laws of your specific state will determine how property, other assets, debts, and spousal and child support will be calculated in the event your marriage ends in divorce. When you marry, the court views the union like a contract where automatic property rights exist for one another. Determining what your specific rights and responsibilities are relative to assets acquired before the union and after can be a very important step in asset protection in the event of divorce or death.

If you are already married, don't worry. You and your spouse can enter into a postnuptial agreement by hiring separate counsel and fully disclosing all of your assets, income, and liabilities. This is a similar document to a prenuptial agreement but the document is signed after you're married.

MYTHS ABOUT PRENUPTIAL AGREEMENTS

Myth #1
THERE IS NO SUCH THING AS AN IRONCLAD PRENUP.

Although courts do invalidate prenuptial agreements in part or in full, normally the ones that are prepared without the help of an attorney or where there is coercion, duress, or lack of disclosure are the ones that often are set aside by courts. If you have a prenuptial agreement that is properly drafted by competent counsel, there is no coercion or duress, and the agreement is fair and equitable, it is likely the prenuptial agreement will be enforced by any court.

Myth #2
ONLY MEN WANT PRENUPTIAL AGREEMENTS.

That is actually not true. A prenuptial agreement is a useful tool to set both partners' expectations for the relationship. In this day and age, the breadwinner does not necessarily have to be the male in the relationship. I've seen many cases where the woman, who plans on staying home and raising the children, insists on a prenuptial agreement that includes alimony provisions and additional monies for her because she will be interrupting her career. There are also times when the woman is the breadwinner in a heterosexual relationship and she demands that her assets be protected in the event of divorce and that her spouse waive rights to alimony. Prenuptial agreements are gender neutral and can help or assist either a male or a female.

Myth #3
PRENUPTIAL AGREEMENTS ARE ONLY FOR THE WEALTHY.

That's not the case. Middle class people draft prenuptial agreements all the time. If done properly, prenuptial agreements don't have to be overly expensive. As a result of the recent economic downturn, many people have drafted prenuptial agreements that divide and allocate debt rather than assets to ensure that one party will not be responsible for the other's liabilities in the event of divorce or death.

Same-Sex Unions

"Love is gender neutral, it attracts all."
—Anonymous

The status of marriage for same-sex couples is in flux in most of the United States and all over the world. Advance premarital planning is a great strategy for same-sex couples to use to establish and understand their legal rights whether they decide to get married or live together.

If you're in a same-sex relationship, it's important to seek counsel from a professional who is knowledgeable in the field. He or she can explain to you the differences between civil unions and same-sex partnerships and advise you vis-à-vis a prenuptial agreement. Let's take a look at the history and evolution of same-sex unions to better understand the law and how it may affect you before you wed or enter into a long-term committed relationship.

It's crucial to understand the difference between the state and federal benefits regarding same-sex marriages. The federal government does not recognize same-sex marriage in the United States. The lack of federal recognition was codified in 1996 by the Defense of Marriage Act. Same-sex marriages are, however, recognized by some individual states. Each state is free to set the conditions for a valid marriage, subject to limits set by the state's own constitution and the US Constitution. Massachusetts became the first state to grant marriage licenses to same-sex couples in 2004. Such licenses are currently granted by six states: Connecticut, Iowa, Massachusetts, New Hampshire, New York, and Vermont. In addition, you can obtain licenses from the District of Columbia (Washington, DC) and the Coquille Indian Tribe in Oregon. Same-sex marriages could be legally performed in California between June 16, 2008, and November 4, 2008, when voters passed Proposition 8 prohibiting same-sex marriages.

States that recognize out-of-state same-sex marriage, but do not grant same-sex marriage licenses include: Rhode Island and Maryland. As of the publication of this book, 41 US states prohibit same-sex marriage via statute or the state's constitution.

Legal Definitions

The following will explain the terms used for same-sex relationships. We'll then take a look at the legal differences between heterosexual couples and same-sex couples and discuss how to implement an agreement for preservation of future financial assets.

SAME-SEX MARRIAGE, also known as gay marriage, is the equivalent of a legal marriage between people of the same sex. In certain states, marriage licenses are issued to same-sex couples. Same-sex marriage is currently recognized in Argentina, Belgium, Canada, Iceland, the Netherlands, Norway, South Africa, Portugal, Spain, and Sweden. Israel doesn't recognize same-sex marriages performed within its borders, but does recognize those performed in foreign jurisdictions. In Brazil, a same-sex couple can convert their civil union to a marriage with approval from a state judge.

In the US, same-sex marriages are not recognized on a federal level, but are recognized in 6 states and one district (see page 127 to find out which ones). Ballot measures are continually introduced on the subject of same-sex marriage, so it's important to keep up on the current status of the law in your state as it is constantly changing.

First recognized in Vermont in 2000, CIVIL UNION is a category of law that was created to extend rights to same-sex couples recognized only in the state where the couple resides. Civil unions can also be referred to as registered partnerships and civil partnerships.

COMMON-LAW MARRIAGE is an informal marriage that is legally recognized in certain jurisdictions as an actual marriage, although no civil or religious ceremony has been performed. A common-law marriage is legally binding in certain states, but has no legal consequence in others.

DOMESTIC PARTNERSHIP is a new category of law that was created to extend rights to unmarried couples, including—but not necessarily limited to—same-sex couples. The laws vary among states, cities, and countries, and it's important to understand the rights and responsibilities in the specific state where the domestic partnership was created. A couple may share a common partnership without being married or having a civil union. Some states confer rights to a partnership that are equal or close to those conferred on a marriage. Domestic partnerships in the United States are determined by each state or local jurisdiction. There is no nationwide consistency on the rights, responsibilities, and benefits accorded domestic partners.

The *Defense of Marriage Act* (DOMA) is a United States law signed by President Clinton on September 21, 1996 whereby the federal government defines marriage as a legal union between one man and one woman. Under the law, no state may be required to recognize a same-sex relationship considered a marriage in another state. DOMA's Section 3 prevents the federal government from recognizing the validity of same-sex marriages. However, the challenge against DOMA is the constitutional requirement expressed in the Full Faith and Credit Clause in Article IV, Section I of the US Constitution, which establishes that states have certain reciprocal obligations to one another, specifically to honor each others "public acts, records, and judicial proceedings." Under this clause, states are generally required to recognize other states' laws unless they are contrary to the public policy of that state. Over half of all US states have updated their state constitutions with legislation containing language that defines marriage as between a man and a woman.

Since DOMA was passed, there has been an increased focus on the legality of same-sex marriage at the state level. Some states have determined that they will not recognize same-sex marriage or civil unions, while others recognize civil unions as more or less equivalent to marriage. The following chart outlines the laws regarding civil unions and same-sex marriage in US states and territories.

CURRENT MARRIAGE STATUTES STATE BY STATE

STATES WITH STATUTES DEFINING MARRIAGE AS BETWEEN ONE MAN AND ONE WOMAN

Alabama	Idaho	Minnesota	South Dakota
Alaska	Illinois	Mississippi	Tennessee
Arizona	Indiana	Missouri	Texas
Arkansas	Iowa	Montana	Utah
Colorado	Kansas	North Carolina	Virginia
Connecticut	Kentucky	North Dakota	Washington
Delaware	Louisiana	Ohio	West Virginia
Florida	Maine	Oklahoma	Wisconsin
Georgia	Maryland	Pennsylvania	Wyoming
Hawaii	Michigan	South Carolina	

STATES WITH CONSTITUTIONAL LANGUAGE DEFINING MARRIAGE

Alabama	Hawaii	Montana	South Dakota
Alaska	Idaho	Nebraska	Tennessee
Arizona	Kansas	Nevada	Texas
Arkansas	Kentucky	North Dakota	Utah
California	Louisiana	Ohio	Virginia
Colorado	Michigan	Oklahoma	Wisconsin
Florida	Mississippi	Oregon	
Georgia	Missouri	South Carolina	

STATES WITH NO LAWS PROHIBITING SAME-SEX MARRIAGE

Connecticut	Iowa	New Jersey	Rhode Island
District of Columbia	Massachusetts	New Mexico	Vermont
	New Hampshire	New York	

STATES THAT PASSED A DOMA CONSTITUTIONAL AMENDMENT IN 2008

Florida	California	Arizona

Hetero vs. Same-Sex Marriage Rights

The most significant difference between heterosexual marriage and civil unions or domestic partnerships is that only marriage between a man and woman offers federal benefits and protections. According to the federal General Accounting Office, more than 1,138 federal rights and 400 state benefits and protections are conferred to US citizens upon entering a heterosexual marriage. These rights and responsibilities apply only to male and female couples, as DOMA defines marriage as between a man and a woman.

Federal benefits include social security benefits, veteran's benefits, health insurance, Medicaid, hospital visitation, estate taxes, inheritance in the absence of a will, retirement savings, pensions, family leave, and immigration law. The civil union or domestic partnership, which is a category of law that was created to extend rights to same-sex couples in certain states, provides legal protection to couples at only the state level.

Accordingly, if a same-sex couple is legally married in one state and works in another state that does not recognize same-sex marriages, then in most cases, the employer would not be required to recognize that marriage or provide spousal benefits. Notably, however, there are some jurisdictions, such as the District of Columbia, which do not authorize same-sex marriages but do recognize same-sex marriages from other states and the attendant rights.

LEGAL CHECKLIST FOR SAME-SEX COUPLES

❥ Determine whether or not the state in which you live recognizes same-sex marriages or domestic partnerships
❥ Consult with counsel to go over your legal options as a couple
❥ Consult with your insurance broker to determine the availability and cost of coverage for same-sex spouses
❥ Consider maintaining both domestic partner benefits and spousal benefits for same-sex couples at your place of employment

A couple in a same-sex relationship or civil union should think about whether or not a prenuptial agreement makes sense to explore. Hetero and same-sex couples face the same challenges and issues vis-à-vis the emotional and financial considerations around prenuptial agreements. But for same-sex couples, additional topics must be addressed and discussed in detail. Research shows that a majority of gay men and lesbians live together in long-term committed relationships at some point in their

ESSENTIAL LEGAL DOCUMENTS FOR SAME-SEX COUPLES

LIVING WILL Also known as an *advance directive*, this is a legal document prepared by an attorney detailing what types of life-sustaining measures can be utilized when you are unable to make your own medical decisions. It is an important document because in most jurisdictions, lack of one allows your family members to make life-changing decisions on your behalf without your partner's consent or approval.

POWER OF ATTORNEY There are generally two types of powers of attorney, one being financial in nature the other medical. The Financial POA (as it is generally called) appoints the person or persons in charge of all of your finances, bill paying, and accounting in the event you become incapacitated or undergo a medical emergency that renders you unable to make reasonable decisions for yourself. A medical POA (also known as a *durable power of attorney* or *health proxy*) is a legally prepared document that names a specific person in charge of your medical condition in the event you become incapacitated. Without this, family members or a court guardian may be the ones making life-changing decisions on your behalf.

WILL A Will and Last Testament is the best and most effective legal document to ensure your assets are passed down to whomever you want. When you have a legal will, no one else can dictate where your assets wind up. If you die without a will in a same-sex relationship, civil union, or domestic partnership, your assets may not legally pass to your partner. Drafting and updating your will from time to time as needed will ensure inheritance for your partner and protect the integrity of your relationship under inheritance laws in the event of your death.

life (Black, Gates, Sanders and Taylor, 2000). With that in mind, drafting a cohabitation agreement may make good sense. You can protect your finances, determine who will pay for what, and specify who can inherit what from whom, thus creating a family plan for future financial security.

Clearly understanding the legal restrictions on same-sex couples is crucial to your plan. Be proactive and learn the laws in your home state and how you can best take advantage of the rights afforded to you and your partner. It is also important to review your estate plan with your partner and get the proper legal advice to determine whether or not it makes sense to draft a living will, power of attorney for finances and healthcare, and a will or trust.

Couples who live in places where civil unions or domestic partnerships aren't recognized may voluntarily enter into a private, informal, domestic partnership agreement or cohabitation agreement, specifying their mutual obligations. However, this involves drawing up a number of separate legal documents, including wills, power of attorney, healthcare directives, and child custody agreements, and is best done with the guidance of competent counsel. Regardless, any way you choose to live with your partner, you can make it work and do it with proper premarital planning.

If you want to adopt a child or children as a couple, it's critical to determine where gay adoption is legally permissible. Are you thinking about adopting from the US or overseas? Next, ask each other if adopting is right for you both. Are you in agreement about bringing a child into your family? Do you both have the time and financial capability to raise a child? Educate yourselves about the costs of adoption and whether or not you wish to have an open or closed adoption, a situation in which your names and details of the adoption are kept private. Consider foster care or artificial insemination.

Look into all possibilities if you want build a family together. Gay couples may legally adopt in most states, but many states have different rules and regulations for gay adoption. With the aid of a competent counselor, attorney, and an adoption agency, decide what fits best for you and your partner. This is a huge undertaking and discussing all of the important components will make for a better, stronger bond to raise a child.

SAME-SEX UNION QUESTIONNAIRE

1. What do you expect when we move in together?

   MY RESPONSE _____

   _____

   YOUR RESPONSE _____

   _____

2. Are you ready to discuss marriage?
   In which state would we wed?

   MY RESPONSE _____

   YOUR RESPONSE _____

3. Where can we legally marry? Is domestic partnership or civil union
   the right path if we can't wed in our home state? What rights will
   be afforded to us in a same-sex marriage, civil union, or domestic
   partnership?

   MY RESPONSE _____

   _____

   YOUR RESPONSE _____

   _____

4. Are you ready to commit to this relationship 100 percent?

   MY RESPONSE _____

   _____

   YOUR RESPONSE _____

   _____

5. What role will religion play in our relationship?

MY RESPONSE _____

_____

YOUR RESPONSE _____

_____

6. How do you want to approach financial security and ownership/ distribution of assets?

MY RESPONSE _____

_____

YOUR RESPONSE _____

_____

7. How will inheritance and estate issues impact each of us in the event that one of us dies?

MY RESPONSE _____

_____

YOUR RESPONSE _____

_____

8. Are children an option in our future? Will we each keep our own health insurance? Does your workplace offer family leave if we adopt or have children?

MY RESPONSE _____

_____

YOUR RESPONSE _____

_____

9. How will our families support our union?
   How can we help improve familial relations with our respective families?

   MY RESPONSE _____

   _____

   YOUR RESPONSE _____

   _____

10. Why do we want to spend the rest of our lives together?
    Jot down your top two reasons.

    MY RESPONSE _____

    _____

    YOUR RESPONSE _____

    _____

When the Honeymoon IS OVER

Long-term strategies for a happy, healthy union

Basic Rules and Skills for a Successful Marriage

**You don't marry someone you can live with,
you marry the person you cannot live without.
—Anonymous**

The beginning months of a marriage can feel effortless and exciting, but marriages require attention and often the ability to compromise by both partners if they're to be successful in the long term. You'll need to build healthy habits that will serve you well over the course of time. There's no question that there will be unexpected challenges along the way that can test the strength and viability of your marriage. While new influences are certain to enter your life and you or your partner may develop new perspectives about things, it's important to welcome change and to work together, rather than be fearful of it. By facing change together, you will be stronger.

When your relationship is going well, it truly does improve your life in every way, including your work and home life, as well as your physical and emotional health. Conversely, there is nothing worse emotionally and physically than a bad relationship. If approached in the right way, working out issues in your marriage can be painless and effortless. If not, it can be emotionally draining and detrimental to the longevity of your relationship. Look at your relationship as an investment. The more work you put into it, the more you will get out of it.

The following are some basic rules that couples should follow in order to ensure a long and happy marriage.

Rules for a Happy Marriage

BE AND REMAIN BEST FRIENDS

Hopefully, before you got married, you created a strong foundation of friendship. The goal is to maintain that as you grow and change as a marital team. Consider the way you treat your best friend—the buddy you go golfing with or your shopping pal. You would never treat that person the way you sometimes treat your partner. Don't give your partner your worst; give him or her your best.

PRESERVE MUTUAL LOVE AND RESPECT

Clearly this is a basic rule for every married couple. But what does it really mean? When you respect somebody's opinions, values, and belief system, you will always be able to artfully disagree on a topic without demoralizing or hurting that person's integrity. Make a vow at the beginning of your marriage to love and respect each other. That vow will invariably be the most important tool you have in keeping your marriage happy and healthy.

PRACTICE FORGIVENESS

We are all human and are fallible. It's important for your spouse to know that you're able to say, "I understand, you made a mistake, and I forgive you." If you cannot forgive each other, your relationship will incur battle wounds. These create anger, resentment, and bitterness down the road, and eventually deplete the resources necessary for a healthy and happy marriage. You also need to be able to apologize and say at times that *you're* wrong, *you're* sorry, and *you* will make amends. During the time I have been practicing law, many clients have told me that their spouses have never been able to say "I'm sorry," and that has caused a rift in their marriage.

PRACTICE UNCONDITIONAL ACCEPTANCE

Once you're married, it's important to understand that you cannot change anybody. You can only change yourself. If you truly accept the person who will be your life partner, that acceptance must be unconditional.

TRUST EACH OTHER

Without trust, your foundation will always be shaky. It is an element of a marriage that needs to be intact at all times. What does trust mean to you? Does it mean reliability? Viability? Loyalty? Or all of the above? I think trust encompasses all of those words. It means that you and your partner are there for each other no matter what. If your spouse says he is going out for milk, you need to believe he's actually going out for milk and not doing something that would jeopardize the marriage.

If you have any concerns about trust issues in your marriage or relationship, you need to make sure that you check in with your spouse now, because if, in fact, there is a question, your marriage cannot last if you are always second-guessing him or her. If the trust issue is really about you, that's another problem that needs to be addressed personally in therapy or with a life coach.

Skills for a Happy Marriage

Knowing the Rules for a Happy Marriage will help, but you'll need skills in order to be able to follow them. Even if you consider yourself to be a good communicator or a good listener in your other relationships, that may not carry over into your relationship with your spouse. Communication, listening, and conflict resolution skills within a marriage tend to be more charged with emotion than in other relationships and can evolve into unhealthy patterns. Working on the following skills will help ensure that the two of you are able to meet the many challenges you're sure to face along the way.

COMMUNICATION

Direct, honest, and assertive communication is crucial. Talk with your partner about your dreams, your goals, your feelings, your needs, your wants, your *everything*. If something isn't going your way or you're upset with your spouse, don't hold it in. Tell him or her there and then. Festering over emotional concerns with your spouse will only spill into other aspects of your life and will deplete your emotional reserves.

I had a friend who never spoke to her husband about her feelings, but would call me to discuss their problems. As a compassionate friend, I always listened, but often wondered why she couldn't communicate with her husband. She would describe to me the reaction she expected from her husband when she raised a tough topic, and chose to stay silent rather than talk the issue through. What do you think happened to her marriage? You guessed it. They divorced and she discovered she had an ulcer from the internal pain she caused herself from holding in her emotions. NEVER do that!

Check in with one another. Even if your lives become hectic with work (and eventually children), it's important to stay tuned in to what's going on with your spouse. Text messaging, e-mailing, Skyping are all ways to keep in contact with the person you love to see what's going on in his or her busy day. I am an old-school romantic and still love to send

---

TALKING POINTS: TIPS TO GET THE DIALOGUE FLOWING

➤ Don't let busy schedules become an excuse. Set aside time each day—whether it's over breakfast, or as you crawl into bed each night—to reconnect.

➤ Realize that we all communicate and respond to communication differently. If your partner is just not getting it, try a different form of communication.

➤ Don't take daily communication for granted. It is the quickest way to resolve potential problems. However, failure to communicate is the quickest way to create them.

TOP TEN COMMUNICATION TIPS FOR A HAPPY MARRIAGE

1. Think before you speak.
2. Don't blame your partner.
3. Be honest.
4. Don't discount your partner's feelings and opinions.
5. Don't overreact.
6. Give your partner complete attention.
7. Never dig up past conflicts.
8. Say "I'm sorry..." and mean it.
9. Compromise.
10. Communicate from a place of love.

written notes and cards. I think everyone loves to receive them, so don't forget that sometimes you can sit down and write a poem or a love letter to the person you love proclaiming your feelings for him or her.

If I've had a bad day, I always try to tell my partner "Hey, listen, I had a really bad day and I just want to be left alone for a little while. I hope you're okay with it, it has nothing to do with you." Once that line of communication is open and my partner knows that my bad mood has nothing to do with him, it diffuses any issue that could arise or anything that I say that may be offensive to him for the entire night. When you're in a bad mood, sometimes you just want to react right away with vitriol. That could snowball into a major fight, discontent, and a terrible evening that could last for days on end. Over time, telling your partner how you really feel and what's going on with you can make the difference between a happy marriage and a broken one.

LISTENING

Being a good listener is perhaps the most important skill you can develop for a successful marriage. Many people take listening for granted. They often confuse it with merely paying attention. But true listening is an active endeavor. If you're not participating, you might as well be wearing earplugs. Listening is the ultimate sign of respect while not listening is the ultimate sign of disrespect. I can't tell you the number of clients who said to me "My partner never listened to me or was always busy doing something else (such as texting) while I was talking." It's obvious the clients just wanted to be heard.

Shut off your phone, TV, or radio, and sit one-on-one and talk and listen. There is nothing better than old-fashioned conversation. You can talk about your thoughts, fears, and challenges of the day, and how to tackle them collectively. Or, you can just hear what your partner has to say. Sometimes he or she may just need a sounding board. It really doesn't cost anything and truly enhances relationships when you pay attention, look your partner in the eye, and listen. One of my clients told me that taking long walks together with no outside distractions, such as cell phones and iPods, greatly improved their marriage. They held hands, were attentive and focused on one another, shared nature all around, and even lost some weight together.

Listening is a two-way street. We all know people who just talk to hear themselves speak. On the other hand, sometimes it's what you're *not* saying that matters. Reading between the lines is something that you can do only if you intently listen to your spouse. The bottom line with listening skills is that it's crucial to develop them early on in a relationship. The good news is that you can start right now by merely opening your ears and paying more attention. You don't have to take a class in how to listen more effectively—just simply open your ears and pay attention.

Here are some other important tips to being a good listener.

1. Look into your speaker's eyes.

2. Empathize by either nodding, or saying "Yes, I understand."

3. Don't interrupt. People need to have a fluid thought process when they're speaking and it's extremely annoying and frustrating to be interrupted.

4. Ask a follow-up question to ensure that the speaker knows you're hearing what he or she is saying.

5. Ask the speaker if he or she would like any feedback or thoughts regarding the conversation.

6. Make sure you maintain positive body language. Don't cross your arms or turn away from the speaker. These postures show that you're far away from the conversation rather than being engaged in it.

7. And lastly, ask your partner, "Do you feel better? Is there anything else I can do to help you? I really heard what you said and understand what you are going through."

Following these actions will allow your partner to feel comfortable, relaxed, loved, and engaged. It just takes some selfless behavior, focus, and attention on the person that you love. When your partner knows and really feels that you're listening, your relationship will continue to blossom and grow each day. It also increases your partner's confidence to know that he or she has a supportive partner in good and bad times. It isn't always easy to practice active listening but once you get good at this skill, it's truly one of the keys that allows your ongoing relationship to strengthen dramatically.

TIPS FOR TURNING ON THE LOVE HEARING AID

❥ Really listen to your partner—you can't listen and speak simultaneously.

❥ Don't plan your rebuttal while you're actively listening.

❥ Afford your partner the same courtesy you would expect to receive when speaking to him or her.

❥ Be present to listen to, not just hear, your partner.

❥ Turn off all distractions and focus 100 percent on your partner.

CONFLICT RESOLUTION

Marriages have their highs and lows. At times, there's no way to avoid an argument, but you can certainly try to do it respectfully and maturely. When a conflict arises, it's important not to yell. Try to speak calmly and in an unthreatening manner. An argument comes down to figuring out what you can do for your partner to make it clear that you understand what he or she is going through, and that you will try to change your behavior in the future. The silent treatment has never been a productive method in the divorces that I have seen. It causes the issue to fester and creates more animosity and resentment between two people.

If you have a disagreement, it's very important to communicate about the problem at hand, and I mean the *real* problem, not the underlying issue that's been festering for a year. When you're arguing or fighting with your spouse or significant other, the challenges that arise are generally emotionally driven. It is important to try, to the best of your ability, to shelve the emotion and try to resolve the issue. Don't take offense at a problem that exists, and don't allow your ego to get in the way of trying to find a resolution when a serious issue arises. Leave the emotional baggage out of it.

MARRIAGE CONFLICT DON'TS

➤ Don't humiliate, condemn, or attack your partner.

➤ Don't run away, hide, or pretend that there are no real issues.

➤ Don't guilt-trip or manipulate your spouse into believing that he or she is wrong.

➤ Don't project and play the blame game when you have your own personal challenges you need to deal with as well.

➤ Don't generalize during an argument, saying, "You are never here to help me," or "You always do that." Those broad generalizations can be very damaging to a person.

GETTING HELP WITH A CONFLICT

If you are fighting often and you can't determine how to resolve your disputes or come to a fair compromise, there are ways to find assistance. Ask a mutual friend or a family member who has both your best interests at heart to serve as mediator. There are also great counselors, therapists, and relationship coaches who can assist a couple before they are married and during their marriage. Most of my clients have gone to marriage counseling and/or separate counseling at one point or another. Therapists can be very effective at resolving a wide variety of issues and problems that go back to the way a person was raised. Life coaches offer counseling over the phone, so if you're a busy working person or don't have the ability to actually physically go see a therapist you can get help on the phone in the comfort of your own home. The amount of money you spend on a therapist will be invaluable for your future health and sanctity of the marriage that you want to last forever.

Speaking the truth in a nonthreatening manner can resolve a problem efficiently. For example, instead of calling your partner a jerk because he didn't say anything about the way you look in your new dress, say "I really love it when you compliment me about the way I look when I'm wearing something new." That indicates to your spouse that it's time to notice you. Many times we think a compliment, but we don't actually say the words out loud. It's important to try to push yourselves to do those kinds of things. When somebody feels good about him or herself, he or she is more open and is less apt to be confrontational when a small issue arises.

Another way to express your discontent or your hurt feelings in a nonthreatening way is to say, "When you do or say _____, I feel _____." When you talk about feelings, no one can be right or wrong. It's not about winning. It's about what has been said, and how it hurts the other person.

When you're having a disagreement, make sure it's an appropriate time when both of you are alone and have the ability to focus. Try not to have an argument right before you're walking into a play or right before your child's little league game. It's also important to have a safe place to disagree. If you're fighting in a restaurant or a public place, you won't take risks and speak honestly and openly about the issues.

Fight fair. Certain words should always be off limits. I am not a big fan of cursing or demoralizing another person with any negative verbiage. It's one thing to say you hate the way your partner is acting or behaving. It's another thing to say you hate him or her. Those words can never be forgotten.

Be sensitive to the timing of an argument. Pregnancy, menopause, or the postpartum period can be emotional times that can trigger an over-reaction during a disagreement. If your partner has lost his or her job, you may not want to argue about money at that time.

ANGER

Anger is an emotion that I see all too often during the course of the divorce process. Tempers flare and raw nerves are exposed. Piecing the relationship history together, it often turns out that anger was an issue throughout their union and not just an isolated issue that surfaced during the divorce.

Anger is a strong emotion that often goes hand-in-hand with love. Those who we love the most have the power to make us the happiest and the angriest that we've ever felt. The key to defusing anger is conflict management, which gives you the opportunity to implement strategies to respond positively to a situation and reduce conflict as much as possible.

If anger is an issue in your relationship, telling yourself that it's not, or burying the issue with denials and excuses, will only make matters worse. Conflict resolution is a way to address anger (or any issue for that matter) head on so that you not only discuss it, but also learn how to control it. Being proactive by knowing what triggers your anger is also critical. Openly discussing hot-button issues with your partner while things are going well is another way to stave off (or at least minimize) pitfalls down the road.

Laying out these concerns at the inception of a marriage is a great way to nip the issues in the bud, instead of just sweeping them under the rug. You can deal with the underlying cause of your negative feelings toward your partner, ignore them, continue to be in denial, or express your anger in a respectful manner and then ultimately forgive your partner. Remember, anger is really guilt turned inward, so try to identify if you're angry at something your partner did or said, or if it's really just your own baggage that you're carrying around.

Anger comes in many forms and affects men and women differently at different stages in their relationship. Some use it as a way to manipulate or manage others, while some use it as a form of control. If you experience anger, work on establishing limits and boundaries and try to break the old patterns. Controlling anger-related behavior can really save a marriage that seems to be jeopardized or compromised based upon the issues that you hold within.

Conflict is a normal part of married life. Each person has different expectations of a spouse in a relationship, and your interests and desires may vary greatly. When these differences lead to some type of disagreement or confrontation, it's important to resolve the issue in the smartest and most effective way. Marital conflict can be a good thing. It can challenge us to grow as human beings, mature the relationship, and accept change as a positive rather than a negative. But it's not always easy to try to diffuse conflict. Following these tips can help you stop a conflict before it becomes a major catastrophe.

1. Deal with the issue at hand. Focus on the current, relevant conflict. Don't bring up old issues and grudges or attack your spouse during the argument. When you put your partner on the defensive it's very difficult for him or her to see your point of view. So make your argument more about the way you were hurt by a behavior and action rather than projecting the blame.

2. Avoid character assassination. Derogatory words hurt, and when you make your partner feel inadequate by saying something negative about him or her personally, or his or her family, I can assure you the comment won't be forgotten and will contribute to resentment in the long run. If you want to work through conflict,

talk about the behavior of a person. Don't attack the person's character or being.

3. Fight privately. Never air your dirty laundry in front of others, especially children or family, unless you both agree that it is important for a family member to get involved in some capacity. Make sure that you argue or disagree privately; you are the only people who can resolve the issue. No one else is living your life, and when you tell other people about your fights, or they hear about them, things can get twisted. You don't want people knowing bits and pieces of an argument and talking about it to others. It is your marriage, and many things should remain confidential, especially when you might be saying things that you really don't mean while in the heat of the moment.

4. Prevention is better than cure. Always try to preempt an argument wherever possible. When you know that your partner does something that you dislike, perhaps you can advise him or her that you really would appreciate it if he or she would stop so that you don't have the same argument over and over.

5. Don't try to mind-read. If you're not completely sure about what your partner said or meant, ask for clarification. When you assume you know something you don't, it creates a misunderstanding that can lead to major problems.

6. Retreat with dignity. After a disagreement, it's important to not hold a grudge. Walk away with your head high and move on. Never go to bed angry. Never leave your relationship vulnerable by keeping issues open-ended. Make sure you resolve whatever disagreement you have. Take the time you need to heal, but honestly and openly accept that the fight is over. Don't bring it up again in the future, as hard as this may be.

7. Don't judge your spouse. Try to accept your spouse unconditionally and try to understand where he or she is coming from. Some

behavior can trigger a bad memory of childhood that needs to be worked on before a behavioral change can be made. Never laugh or scoff at another person while you are fighting. You don't know what your partner has been through in life and you wouldn't want someone to do the same to you.

EMPATHY

Whenever you or your spouse are going through a difficult time, and it's not affecting you as much as it does your spouse, it's important to have compassion and empathy for the person you love, even if you can't fully understand it at that very moment. Try reversing roles and think about the attention and compassion *you* need when you are going through a difficult time. Make sure that you're there for your spouse emotionally, 100 percent, in good and bad times. It can make the difference between marriage and divorce.

COMPROMISE

It's not so easy to meet your spouse halfway if you feel that you're right and he or she is wrong. But it's really not about who's right and who's wrong. It's important to remove your ego from many of the situations that arise in a marriage. So many couples fail and ultimately get divorced because individuals can't compromise and can't see past their own emotional baggage. Part of the recipe for a successful marriage is to be able to shelve those emotions to the best of your ability, and to see your spouse's point of view. When you do, it will change the landscape of your marriage.

Life is like walking on a tightrope—the give and take can at times be challenging. When it's no longer just you you're thinking about, it can be downright daunting. However, when you compromise, it inevitably gives you a new and fresh perspective on something you may not have tried before. I never thought I would like classical music, taking long walks in Central Park, or running together. But guess what? I do now. We all lead such busy lives. Finding different ways to enjoy new things together brings you closer and solidifies the marital foundation.

SENSE OF HUMOR

Nothing's more important than keeping a healthy dose of humor in your relationship. Laughing together and having jokes that only you and your partner know can help alleviate the daily pressures of life. There's nothing better than laughter to release tension when you've had a stressful day. We all get cranky and irritable at times. All it takes is a good joke on a bad day to shift the mood.

FINDING YOUR STRENGTH IN DIFFICULT TIMES
By Dr. David

Listen. I have some wonderful advice for you. Just listen. Listen. When other people are talking, let them express their thoughts, their opinions and their feelings, especially their feelings. Don't just let them talk. Listen to what they are saying. Pay attention. Try to understand. Listen. You don't have to agree. As a matter of fact, whether you agree or not should be beside the point. Don't express your opinions or feelings while someone else is expressing his or hers. Do you have a problem with that? Do you feel you need to express your opinion? That you must make your feelings known? When others are speaking you won't be heard anyway and you'll just lose points for trying. Listen without waiting for an opportunity to give your side or pounce on the other person or correct his or her mistakes. The other person's reasoning and information are surely full of mistakes and distortions. So what? So are yours. Listen in sincere silence. You don't need to prove your point. Just listen. Everyone thinks a good listener is smart. Listen. You don't need to persuade the other person, just understand. If you don't, ask, can you explain that? Or, what do you really mean? But don't give your opinion while the other person is talking. Just let him or her talk. The good listener hears the unspoken thought. Listen for it. When the other person is finished, mention that inner thought. The other person will know you heard and understood. Then the situation will become quiet because the other person will be listening to your hearing. All the pressure will fade and you can get on with life. Listen. There is nothing quite like being heard.

UNDERSTANDING YOUR PARTNER'S EMOTIONAL CUES

Everyone reacts differently to the way they receive information. Once you get to know the person you're with, you'll know if he or she is in a good or bad mood on any given day. You'll know if he wants to be left alone or she wants to cuddle. These nonverbal cues, such as eye contact, body language, or facial expressions speak a thousand words. Become receptive to nonverbal cues and understand how to send and receive communication during a difficult time. When your partner is upset with you and you go to give him or her a hug, does he or she immediately move or push you away? That's an important red flag to note.

FUN

Being able to have fun as a couple is one of the most important skills needed to sustain a long marriage. Isn't it great when you and your partner have things that you like to do and you look forward to doing them together? Do you like to go to the movies? Do you like to ride your bikes? Do you like to walk around downtown and look at art galleries? Whatever it may be, find those fun things you can do together and enjoy each other's company. Keep it light, make it happy, and focus on laughing together. When you can do that, you're guaranteed a sustainable marriage.

Now you have the basic rules and skills necessary for a thriving, happy marriage. Review the Ten Marital Commandments (page 168) and begin to really focus on what it's going to take to make your marriage last forever.

Keeping the Flame Alive

"Passion is the quickest to develop
and the quickest to fade.
Intimacy develops more slowly and
commitment more gradually still."
—Robert Stern Berg

I've spoken to many married couples about their intimacy challenges. Many say that after a few months of marriage, or a few years, the level of intimacy wanes because partners begin to lose focus on each other and focus more on children and work. That's an understandable excuse. It's important that you work to earn a living during the day. But we can't allow our daily routines—which include career, children, or financial responsibilities—to douse the flame. Setting aside time each week to make sure you and your partner receive pleasure together on an emotional and sexual level is part and parcel of maintaining a thriving, healthy intimate life. Did you know that adults on average have sex with their partners about 60 times per year according to the University of Chicago's National Opinion Research Center? As a marriage ages, sexual relations between spouses dramatically decline. In fact, the same opinion research center showed that in longer marriages, the frequency could be as low as 16 times per year.

You and your partner should feel comfortable with, and mutually agree on, what it takes to keep your relationship on the highest intimate level. Keep in mind, also, that true intimacy goes beyond the bedroom. A gentle touch on the cheek and a hug at the door are simple gestures, but they keep the spark alive. Couples need to reprioritize their busy lives to take time for love, intimacy, and sex. A subpar or nonexistent sex life can cause great strife and a major disconnection in any marriage.

Consider these tips on how to stay in a healthy, sexually secure marriage. Dr. Belissa Vranich, creator of the *More Love, Less Handles Workout* suggests that shared activities (as opposed to similar interests) can keep your love alive. Dr. Belissa states that one of the best ways to spend time together is through working out, which offers far more than just physical benefits. Working out can create longer and more fulfilling relationships. You've heard it said that couples that play together, stay

---

ANNIVERSARIES, BIRTHDAYS, ENGAGEMENTS, SPECIAL PLACES

Always remember those special days and places you and your partner shared together. Remember the first place you kissed? Or the day you became engaged? Or your wedding anniversary, which is so often overlooked or forgotten? Make sure you jot these dates down in a calendar that automatically repeats yearly. Plan something special and unique before a special occasion. It doesn't matter if you're a man or woman, in a heterosexual relationship, or in a same-sex union. Being thoughtful is gender neutral. Being kind is a requirement for a loving marriage.

Just think about the joy it gives your partner when you give him a special gift on an anniversary or when you take her to dinner at her favorite restaurant. It takes a little planning to make the person you love happy. Isn't it worth it?

I see so many couples overlooking these small landmarks. Remembering them boosts closeness and love in a marriage. Don't be too busy in your day to put your partner first. I always have several calendars that mark important dates in my personal life in addition to my business and work dates. Make sure your personal calendar is up-to-date and accessible at all times. Whether you like the old-fashioned desk ones, or use a computer-organized calendar linked to your phone, be sure to set crucial dates in a place and set to notify you a week in advance. We are all caught up in the busy day at work, with children, or caring for others. The person that gets the least attention is sometimes your partner. When you can't remember the last time you bought a gift or wrote a card for your honey, take a step back. Complacency in a marriage is a disaster waiting to happen.

together. This could not be truer when it comes to having shared activities and exercise, which is one of the easiest things you can do to reap physical and emotional benefits.

About an hour after you've exercised, endorphins (the feel-good chemicals) are released. If you spent that time exercising with your partner, you will psychologically feel more connected and attracted to him or her. Engaging in eye contact, reading each other's facial expressions, and pushing each other to your physical limits will improve the way you relate emotionally in all ways. It can also help in conflict resolution. When you argue, your body becomes physically tense, and that tension needs to be released. Dr. Belissa's advice is to stop talking about it and go work out together. Regardless of how mad you may be, you'll notice a big difference once your body releases its tension and anger through exercise. Communication will become much easier and resentment won't build up as readily as it did before you were physically active.

There's nothing like feeling confident in the bedroom after you've exercised and are feeling good about the way your body looks in the mirror. If you're confident about your body and your outward appearance, you'll have less insecurity and welcome your partner's touch. Caution: if you're obsessed about the way you look, that can also lead to a disaster in the bedroom and may require some therapy for help on the underlying issues.

Try to maintain a fit and healthy appearance. I've heard many of my past clients complain that either their spouses had gained weight or had let themselves go. You never want to be that person, because you always want your spouse or partner to be attracted to you physically as well as emotionally. It doesn't matter what size you are. If you feel good about yourself, your partner will be attracted to you. There is no reason that two people who are in love should not remain in love and attracted to each other for years and years to come. If you fail to pay attention to this part of your marriage, you may be heading for infidelity.

Some researchers have said that there's a 50/50 chance that one partner will cheat in a marriage. Here are some facts and information about infidelity that you may find interesting.

- Spouses who are unfaithful are most likely to start cheating three to five years into their marriage.

- Having children does not protect against infidelity. Couples with young children engage in infidelity as frequently as married couples without children.

- Even couples that are head-over-heels in love at the beginning of a relationship may find themselves in a position where infidelity may strike because intense feelings of love change over time.

Gender differences influence cheating and play an important role in a relationship. Ask the following questions of your spouse:

1. What is your past sexual history?
2. How attracted are you to me?
3. How much time do you spend online recreationally?
4. How many same-sex friends do you have, and why?

Another factor that may contribute to the increased chance of infidelity is marital dissatisfaction. Those who say their relationships aren't too happy are four times more likely to engage in infidelity than those who say they're very happy (Michael R. T. Gagnon, J. H. Laumann, Edward O. Kolata, Gina (1995) *Sex In America: A Definitive Survey,* Boston: Little, Brown, 1995.)

Be very cognizant of the friendships that you make outside of your marriage, and be clear on the need and the reason for your relationships. Are you relying as heavily on a friend or a coworker as on your partner? If you are a male, do you have only female employees around you who are young and attractive? Does that send the wrong signal in the work place or at home? Do you find yourself e-mailing and texting a work friend constantly, and thinking about him or her while you're at home? Examine your friendships from time to time. Try to understand why you prefer certain ones, which may indicate that your marital relationship is lacking in some way. You may be trying to compensate for what might be lacking with a friendship that crosses unhealthy lines. This is how infidelity gets started.

You need to create boundaries with your friends outside of the home to ensure that you are exactly that—friends and nothing more. Marriage means no playing around or fooling around *ever* with anyone outside the relationship unless you both agree. Most conventional marriages don't have room for another person in the bedroom. Fantasies do not equate to infidelity. Anyone can dream and fantasize, but actually creating a behavior that crosses the line certainly enters murky waters.

Putting Your Partnership First

So when you think about life with your significant other, who pops into your head first? You or your partner? When you think about life choices, do you only want the best for yourself, or do your partner's wishes and dreams mean as much or even more to you? I often think the way we are raised teaches us to worry about ourselves first. I love the concept of taking care of yourself, but what about the ones you love? If you already have a child, the answer is easy. Most spouses think of their children first, then each other. I'm not so sure that's the correct order. I think your child or children should be on the same level as your significant other. That way, there is less animosity, less manipulation, and love can be shared equally. That's not to say a child doesn't need a parent more in the beginning years of life. It only means that putting your partner before you can lead to an amazing, selfless marriage.

Making your spouse a priority in your mind and a priority on paper are two different things. You can say your spouse is a top priority, but do you make sure to schedule time to spend with him or her? Each spouse may have a different definition of how you connect as a couple. Make sure that you both feel you are reconnecting (Tim Downs, author of the book *Fight Fair*).

When you get into a pattern of putting your partnership first, it becomes exciting, fun, and incredibly rewarding. The joy that you see from your partner will make your heart sing and rejoice.

Daily Love Log

The first thing I do when I wake up is make a to-do list for my day. Usually it's comprised of work-related goals, some errands, and a few things on my love list. I think of how I can help my partner with his day. I try to think of ways to help him grow and support his life goals. I think about how I can make his day easier and what he needs from me to help get through a tough challenge. I always make sure I maintain constant communication, to stay in touch. You may not be able to access your phone, so e-mail may be a better option for you. Whatever mode of communication works for you, stay in touch in some capacity. Without this, you lose touch with the inner workings of your partner—who he or she is in contact with, what he or she is feeling, going through, etc. It's like two strangers being married, or a shell without the tortoise inside. It doesn't work for the marriage you strive for.

IDEAS FOR CELEBRATING SPECIAL OCCASIONS

❧ Go camping. Pack strawberries and chocolate. Get your own tent. Although this might seem grimy, trust me it's the most fun and sexy way to spend a secluded night with your partner.

❧ Send a text hunt telling your partner where to meet you with clues… its fun, cute, and wildly sexy.

❧ Cook your partner his or her favorite dinner or have it ordered in. The little things go so far in life.

❧ Have a picnic if camping isn't for you. Pack cheese, crackers, wine, and a blanket. Don't forget your dog, if you have one. It's a fun, simple, and inexpensive way to spend quality time with the person you love on a special day.

Your Happily Ever After

"A successful marriage requires
falling in love many times,
always with the same person."
—Mignon McLaughlin

Recently, I was out at dinner with my family and I saw a lovely elderly couple sitting adjacent to us. They were acting so sensitively and warmly toward one another, I felt compelled to strike up a conversation. I asked the gentleman if they were having a nice dinner, and he told me that we were at his wife's favorite restaurant. She turned to him and said "I would hope that you know me by now. We've only been married for 65 years." That struck me as amazing. It's always heartwarming to see a couple happily married for an extended period of time.

"How did you meet, if you don't mind me asking?" I wondered aloud.

The wife said that they had been high school sweethearts.

"What's your secret?" I quizzed "Please tell." I explained to them what I do for a living.

They actually giggled and said, "Wow, you have a tough job. We're glad we never got to see you during our lifetime." Then they said three very important things.

1. Choose your battles wisely.
2. Love each other through good and bad times.
3. Make time for one another to talk and listen.

I was so impressed by this couple that I couldn't focus on my family during dinner. I wanted to continue to ask them more questions, but didn't want to be too intrusive. I noticed them being loving and kind to one another. They shared their meals with each other and the wife even took a napkin and wiped her husband's face because he had some salmon stuck on his cheek. For me, they epitomized a long-lasting love, which is what I am trying to envision for you.

This special time in your life is sure to evoke feelings of joy, a bit of nervousness, and pure excitement. Those are very common feelings when you're considering marriage or are newly wed. After reading this book and taking your premarital planning seriously, you're better equipped to cope with whatever life throws in the way of your marriage. You have done what most couples, unfortunately, do not do, and that is work on issues before you wed. You and your partner were willing participants to better understand how each other ticks, and this will bring you closer for the long haul, and not just for your wedding. You are committed to making your marriage the best it can be. You understand that a marriage takes work. You know that after the honeymoon, life resumes as normal. But a loving, committed relationship requires that you apply all of the basic marital skills you've acquired in order for your marriage to flourish. You now have the necessary foundation to cultivate a happy and healthy lasting marital union.

You have surely gained insight about your partner from the interactive charts and questionnaires that you both filled out. You can compare your answers and see what topics you need to improve upon. I'm sure you learned more about proper communication, listening skills, and money discussions. You have learned about techniques for keeping intimacy alive, dealing with conflict, proceeding with prenuptial planning, and gaining skills that will make living together go more smoothly from the onset. Hopefully, you now know which one of you wants children and whether or not living together is a good idea. You may understand your role in your relationship and what expectations your partner has that you may have been unaware of before. I hope I have given you the tools and strategies that you didn't have before picking up this book. I hope that you live by the 10 Marital Commandments (see page 168).

I want you to join the millions of couples living in happy, monogamous marriages forever.

Don't be surprised if, after reading this book you find yourself referring to certain chapters when challenges arise in your marriage. One of the many purposes of this book is to serve as a reference. Don't read it and then tuck it away in a box. Keep it on your bookshelf or your nightstand. Reread it as needed. Fill out the questionnaires yearly with your partner to see how you both have changed and grown together as a couple. As you and your partner evolve as individuals, so will your marriage. Be cognizant of the fact that there may be some growing pains along the way. That's normal. The way you work on them in a loving, caring fashion is what will set you apart in the long run in regard to happiness and success in your marriage. You will have to work hard at resolving those inevitable, but easily surmountable, issues. No one that I have ever spoken to promises that marriage is easy. In fact, it has been described as a labor of love, an art form of sorts, where you must use the skills necessary to be a loving partner every day of your life. Some days won't be as easy as others, but if you implement the tools in this book and really work at it, you will have developed the keys to a happy and successful marriage. You will be a role model for those around you and your children in the future. That gift will be one of the most important life lessons that one can share. May love and happiness always surround you. You have one life to live. Why not share it with the love of your life in a sustaining, abundant, and loving marriage?

HAPPY
MARRIAGE
Resources

Marital Action Plan

Follow these guidelines and your marriage is sure to be on the road to longevity.

1. Trust

2. Show gratitude

3. Emit emotion

4. Show recognition

5. Love kindly

6. Maintain honesty at all times

7. Show loyalty

8. Talk lovingly and with deep respect

9. Support without hesitation

10. Touch often

10 Marital Affirmations

Read these affirmations together with your partner and on your own. They will help you focus on and remind you about your goals for your relationship.

1. I am in a loving marriage.

2. I trust that I am always in marital bliss.

3. I love to give and receive love.

4. Our marriage works effortlessly.

5. My love flows effortlessly.

6. Our commitment to each other is unwavering.

7. We cherish the journey we share together.

8. My love ignites our passion and joy.

9. I am so grateful for my loving partner.

10. I embrace the love I share with my partner.

10 Marital Commandments

Read these commandments together and reread them monthly. Hold yourself and your partner accountable to keeping these commandments.

1. Unconditionally love your partner always.

2. Respect your partner always.

3. Compliment your partner often.

4. Commit to your partner unequivocally.

5. Honor the sanctity of marriage.

6. Support your partner without question during good and bad times.

7. Work on strengthening the bond that you and your partner have to make it everlasting.

8. Commit to trusting your partner without hesitation indefinitely.

9. Focus on your partner's happiness always.

10. Emotionally and physically consign yourself to your partner unconditionally.

Healthy Marriage Habits

How do relationships contribute to our overall health, if at all? People who have healthy, supportive relationships have a higher quality of life. They also have a higher rate of recovery after illness than individuals who have not cultivated relations in their life that are built upon values, like trust, honesty, and caring intentions.

In recognition of this proven link, the World Health Organization defines health as "a state of complete mental, physical and social well being and not merely the absence of disease or infirmary." (World Health Organization, 2001) Our social support/relationships play a significant role in our health and our ability to recover from debilitating diseases. Therefore, having healthy partnerships and friendships with supportive and kind people can do much to improve not just life in general, but your health as well. We all want to be emotionally and physically well. Using healthy habits in your marriage will be more beneficial than you could ever imagine. Reducing stress in your relationship can produce longevity and happiness, and, let's face it, isn't that all we really want for life? I know that's it for me!

1. You can't change anyone but yourself, so stop trying. Accept your partner for who he or she is or leave.

2. If something doesn't feel right, don't ignore that red flag.

3. Love yourself first. You can't love anyone else until you fully love and accept yourself unconditionally.

4. Be honest and own your stuff. We all have childhood wounds. Don't project them on your partner. Talk about them and create dialogue around how you feel and how your wounds can be healed instead of used against your partner.

5. Put your partner first.

Jot down five healthy relationship habits you want to improve on in your relationship.

_____

_____

_____

_____

_____

What do you think your partner would say about them? What habits are you most proud of? What would he/she say?

_____

_____

_____

_____

_____

Sample Cohabitation Agreement

The following form is intended for illustrative purposes only. You and your attorney can use this sample as a guide in drafting a cohabitation agreement that best protects your interests and complies with the laws in effect where you live.

_____, Cohabitant # 1, and _____, Cohabitant # 2, hereinafter jointly referred to as the Cohabitants, who now live/will live together in the future (circle one) at _____ in the City of _____, County of _____, State of _____, hereby agree on this _____ day of _____, in the year _____, as follows:

1. The Cohabitants wish to establish their respective rights and responsibilities regarding each other's income and property and the income and property that may be acquired, either separately or together, during the period of cohabitation.

2. The Cohabitants have made full and complete disclosure to each other of all of their financial assets, income, and liabilities.

3. Except as otherwise provided below, the Cohabitants waive the following rights:

   a. To share in each other's estates upon their death.

b. To "palimony" or other forms of support or maintenance, both temporary and permanent.

c. To share in the increase in value during the period of cohabitation of the separate property of the parties.

d. To share in the pension, profit sharing, or other retirement accounts of the other.

e. To the division of the separate property of the parties, whether currently held or hereafter required.

f. To any other claims based on the period of cohabitation of the parties.

g. To claim the existence of a common-law marriage.

4. [SET FORTH RELEVANT EXCEPTIONS HERE. For instance, if both cohabitants are contributing to the debt repayment on the home owned by one party, they may agree that any increase in equity during the period of cohabitation will be fairly divided between them.]

5. The Cohabitants agree to divide the household expenses as follows:

MONTHLY EXPENSES

	COHABITANT NO. 1	COHABITANT NO. 2
RENT OR MORTGAGE	_____	_____
UTILITIES		
Telephone	_____	_____
Gas	_____	_____
Electricity	_____	_____

Water & Sewer _____ _____

Garbage Collection _____ _____

Cable Television _____ _____

Cellular Phone _____ _____

Internet Service _____ _____

Property Taxes _____ _____

INSURANCE

Homeowners _____ _____

Renters _____ _____

Auto(s) _____ _____

Recreational Vehicle _____ _____

DEBT PAYMENTS

Vehicle #1 _____ _____

Vehicle #2 _____ _____

Home Equity Loan _____ _____

Other Loans _____ _____

Credit Card #1 _____ _____

Credit Card #2 _____ _____

Credit Card #3 _____ _____

DAY CARE _____ _____

TRANSPORTATION
EXPENSES

Gasoline _____ _____

Parking/Commuting _____ _____

Vehicle Maintenance _____ _____

Licenses _____ _____

FOOD   _____   _____

Groceries   _____   _____

Take-out Food   _____   _____

Restaurants   _____   _____

School Lunches   _____   _____

HOUSEHOLD EXPENSES

Cleaning Supplies   _____   _____

Cleaning Service   _____   _____

Yard Maintenance   _____   _____

Home Maintenance   _____   _____

Home Security   _____   _____

Home Repairs   _____   _____

Home Furnishings   _____   _____

Appliances   _____   _____

PERSONAL EXPENSES

Personal Grooming
and Self-Care   _____   _____

Entertainment   _____   _____

Gifts   _____   _____

Hobbies   _____   _____

Babysitting   _____   _____

Pet-Care Costs   _____   _____

Donations   _____   _____

Other Expenses   _____   _____

TOTAL EXPENSES   _____   _____

6. [ADDITIONAL PROVISIONS HERE]. These can cover just about any issue, from custody of pets to allocating household chores. The legal obligation to pay child support to any children of the Cohabitants cannot, however, be modified by agreement of the parties.]

7. Each Cohabitant is represented by separate and independent legal counsel of his or her own choosing.

8. The Cohabitants have separate incomes and assets to independently provide for their own respective financial needs.

9. This agreement constitutes the entire agreement of the parties and may be modified only in a writing executed by both Cohabitants.

10. In the event it is determined that a provision of this agreement is invalid because it is contrary to applicable law, that provision is deemed separable from the rest of the agreement, such that the remainder of the agreement remains valid and enforceable.

11. This agreement is made in accordance with the laws of the state of _____, and any dispute regarding its enforcement will be resolved by reference to the laws of that state.

12. This agreement will become null and void upon the legal marriage of the Cohabitants.

I HAVE READ THE ABOVE AGREEMENT, I HAVE TAKEN TIME TO CONSIDER ITS IMPLICATIONS, I FULLY UNDERSTAND ITS CONTENTS, I AGREE TO ITS TERMS, AND I VOLUNTARILY SUBMIT TO ITS EXECUTION.

_____   _____
Cohabitant No. 1   Cohabitant No. 2

Witnessed by:

_____   _____
(Witness or counsel signature)   (Witness or counsel signature)

[NOTARY PUBLIC MAY AFFIX STAMP HERE]

Sample Prenuptial Agreement

Disclaimer: This Prenuptial Agreement is a sample standard document that can be utilized for illustrative purposes to determine whether or not it is necessary for you and your partner to enter into a complete comprehensive Prenuptial Agreement. Every Prenuptial Agreement should have an attachment that cites specifically the assets and liabilities that you and your partner have before you enter into the marriage. Specifically, with the name of the asset, the approximate value and who will be maintaining that asset after the marriage takes place.

THIS AGREEMENT is made and entered into on this _____ day of _____, _____ between _____ (hereinafter, _____), prospective Wife, a United States citizen, with an address of _____ and _____, prospective Husband (hereinafter, _____), a United States citizen, residing at _____, collectively the Parties.

WITNESSETH:

WHEREAS, the parties contemplate marriage to each other, such marriage to be solemnized in the near future;

WHEREAS, the parties have represented to each other that each is legally free to marry;

WHEREAS, each party has full knowledge of the approximate and extent of the values of all property, estate, earned income and financial obligations of the Party which property, earnings and financial obligations presently owned, earned and owed by _____ and _____ are itemized on attached SCHEDULE A and SCHEDULE B, which are attached hereto and made a part of this Prenuptial Agreement;

WHEREAS, in anticipation of the contemplated marriage, the Parties desire to establish, fix, limit and determine by this Agreement insofar as it is permissible by law, interests, rights and claims in and to the Party and estate of the other, which accrued to each of them by reason of their anticipated marriage, and do likewise with respect to the rights of the other, including the rights of the Parties to support, alimony, and equitable distribution, or any other rights which the Parties may acquire through the course of their marriage by statute and/or case law in this State, or in any other jurisdiction;

WHEREAS, each Party has consulted with and reviewed this Agreement with independent legal counsel of his or her choosing and each has done so prior to the execution of this Agreement and each has been fully advised of his or her rights and privileges acquired by virtue of the consummation of the anticipated marriage in the event of divorce;

WHEREAS, both Parties have discussed the terms and conditions, and implications of this Agreement and agree that they are fair and reasonable, and have not been caused to executed based on duress, intimidation or any other oral promise that is not expressly herein;

NOW, THEREFORE, it is agreed upon as follows:

1. All property which belongs to each of us as itemized on our Schedules A and B shall forever remain our separate, personal property regardless of any appreciation in value or change in form of our specific assets, and said property shall remain forever free

of claim of the other now and in the future. Separate property is not subject to division between us in the event of divorce or death. Either one of us has the sole right to manage and dispose of his or her separate property any way he or she deems necessary.

2. Any property acquired during the marriage not deemed to be separate property as defined above, shall be treated and deemed as an asset acquired during the marriage. Said marital property will be subject to division between us in the event of divorce and/or death.

3. Any and all debts acquired before the marriage in separate name shall remain that specific person's obligation to repay. Such debt shall be the separate and sole obligation of the party incurring same.

4. Any gifts given by third parties to either spouse during the marriage shall remain that specific person's property without claim or interest from the other.

5. The Parties hereby understand that this potentially could be an alimony case and fully understand that each Party is waiving their right to request alimony from one another whether it be a temporary form before the Parties' divorce in a permanent format based on the Parties' respective incomes at the time they are entering into this Agreement. (This may not be applicable to you. This may be an alimony case and this is something where an attorney would be advising you regarding your obligations and the law of the specific state within which you live, so it is important to make sure that you get proper counsel regarding this specific provision.)

6. Children. Should the Parties have children during their marriage, all support issues relative to the children in the event of the termination of marriage shall be determined by the court within which the parties live and reside with their specific child or children.

7. Each of the Parties to this Agreement desires to dispose of any and all property on death which may belong to him or her as they deem fit and specifically waive their right to an elective share in his or her estate absent this Agreement. Each party shall surrender or forego and release the other Party and his or her estate from any and all intestate interests, right or distributive share which he or she may otherwise be entitled to upon death and specifically waives the right to elect to take against any last will or codicil made by the other pursuant to the provisions of the specific state statute which would govern this prenuptial agreement.

8. The effective date of this Agreement shall become binding and effective only upon the date of marriage. If we do not have such a marriage ceremony as defined legally by the state, this Agreement in all respects shall become null and void.

9. The definition of the termination of marriage shall be the first filing of a complaint for divorce with proper service under the rules of the specific state and jurisdiction.

10. Each party warrants and represents that he or she has made a full and fair disclosure of the assets and financial obligations acquired by either of them up until the date of this execution and those assets and their approximate values have been annexed hereto as Schedules A and B. Each party waives any and all rights to disclosure of the property and financial obligations of the other beyond the disclosure that is attached hereto. The inadvertent failure to list any particular asset or incorrectly estimate any asset shall not render this Agreement null and void.

11. The Parties acknowledge and represent that this Agreement has been executed by them free from persuasion, fraud and undue influence and emotional distress of any kind whatsoever.

12. This Agreement constitutes the entire understanding between the Parties who represent that there have no other representations, warrants or covenants provided by either of the Parties to one another.

13. Both Parties acknowledge that they have had sufficient time to reflect upon this Agreement and consult with counsel to review the terms of the Agreement.

14. This Agreement shall inure to the benefit of both Parties, their heirs and assigns forever.

15. Each Party to this Agreement understands that by signing this document he or she permanently surrenders claims he or she would have otherwise had under _____ state law, including but not limited to claims of income, property, from the separate property of his or her spouse (partner) and inheritance laws.

IN WITNESS WHEREOF, the parties have hereunto set their respective hands and seals the day and year first above written.

_____

WITNESS

_____

WITNESS

STATE OF

COUNTY OF

BE IT REMEMBERED, that on this _____ day of _____, _____, before me, the subscriber, personally appeared _____, who, I am satisfied, is the person named in the within Agreement, and thereupon has acknowledged that she signed, sealed, and delivered the same as her act and deed for the uses and purposes therein expressed.

STATE OF

COUNTY OF

BE IT REMEMBERED, that on this _____ day of _____, _____, before me, the subscriber, personally appeared _____, who, I am satisfied, is the person named in the within Agreement, and thereupon has acknowledged that he signed, sealed, and delivered the same as his act and deed for the uses and purposes therein expressed.

Last Will and Testament

Disclaimer: This Last Will and Testament is only a sample, partial document for instructive purposes, to review before meeting with an estate attorney. A last will and testament can have more information if appropriate to your specific requirements, such as burial instructions and costs, money left for charity and/or grandchildren, and other specific bequests that you may wish to put in writing.

LAST WILL AND TESTAMENT OF_____

I, _____, a resident of the County of _____, State of _____, being of legal age to make this will; being of sound and disposing mind, memory and understanding, do hereby make, publish and declare this to be my Last Will and Testament, hereby revoke, cancel and annul all wills and codicils at any time heretofore made by me.

ITEM I

For information purposes, at the time of this Will, I am married to _____, and have _____ natural born children, namely:

_____

_____.

ITEM II

I direct that all my legally enforceable debts, funeral expenses, expenses of my last illness and administrative expenses, be paid by my Personal Representative from the assets of my estate as soon as practicable after my death.

I direct that all inheritance, transfer, succession and other death taxes, which may be payable with respect to any property includible as a part of my gross estate, shall be paid from my residuary estate, without any apportionment thereof.

ITEM III

All the rest, residue and remainder of my estate, of every nature and kind, which I may own at the time of my death, real, personal and mixed, tangible and intangible, of whatsoever nature and where-soever situated, I give, devise and bequeath to my spouse (partner), _____, providing he/she survives me.

In the event that my spouse (partner) shall predecease me, I give and devise all the rest, residue and remainder of my estate, as aforesaid, to my children, namely:

_____

_____,

equally, share and share alike, or to their issue, in equal share per stirpes.

ITEM IV

If any part or principal of my estate shall become distributable to any beneficiary hereunder who is then under the age of _____ (_____) years, my Personal Representative and Trustee named hereinafter is hereby granted a power of trust, without bond or other undertaking, to hold and administer such property for the benefit of such person until such person shall attain the age of _____ (_____) years, to invest or reinvest such property, to collect the properly allocable thereto, to pay to or apply to the use and benefit of such person so much of the net income as, in my Trustee's sole discretion, is deemed appropriate and to accumulate for the benefit of such person any income not so paid or applied. My Trustee is authorized to pay to or apply to the use and benefit of such person so much of the principal amount of such person's property and accumulations as is deemed appropriate in the sole discretion of my Trustee. Any remaining principal and income shall be paid to such person when he or she attains the age of _____ (_____) years.

ITEM V

I appoint my spouse (partner) _____, as Personal Representative of this Will, with full power and authority to sell, transfer and convey any and all property, real or personal, which I may own at the time of my death, at such time and place and upon such terms and conditions as my Personal Representative may determine, without necessity of obtaining a court order. If my spouse (partner) does not survive me or if he/she fails to qualify or, if having qualified should die, resign or become incapacitated, then in that event I nominate and appoint _____ as successor Personal Representative of this Will and as trustee of any trusts created by this Will, with all the powers and duties afforded my Personal Representative herein.

I direct that no Personal Representative or Trustee nominated and appointed by me shall be required to furnish any bond or other security for the faithful performance of his or her duties, notwithstanding any provision of law to the contrary.

ITEM VI

Failing the survival of my spouse (partner) as natural guardian I appoint _____ or failing him/her I appoint _____ to be the legal Guardian of my minor children named:

_____

_____,

until such time as they attain _____ years of age. Said Guardian shall not be required to furnish security for acting in this capacity.

IN WITNESS WHEREOF, I have hereunto subscribed my name and affixed my seal at the City of _____, State of _____, this _____day of _____, _____, in the presence of the subscribing witnesses who I have requested to become attesting witnesses hereto.

_____(SEAL)

Testator/Testatrix

This instrument was, on the date hereof, signed, published and declared by _____, to be his/her Last Will and Testament, in our presence and in the presence of each of us and we, at the same time, at his/her request, in his/her presence and in the presence of each other, have hereunto signed our names and addresses as attesting witnesses.

_____ of _____
         Witness   Address

_____ of _____
         Witness   Address

State of

County of

We, _____,
and _____, the Testator/Testatrix, and the witnesses, respectively, whose names are signed to the attached and foregoing instrument, being first duly sworn, do hereby declare to the undersigned officer that the Testator/Testatrix signed the instrument as his/her Last Will and Testament and that he/she signed voluntarily and that each of the witnesses, in the presence of the Testator/Testatrix, at his/her request, and in the presence of each other, signed the Will as a witness and that to the best of the knowledge of each witness the Testator/Testatrix was at that time eighteen or more years of age, of sound mind and under no constraint or undue influence.

_____

Testator/Testatrix

_____

Witness

_____

Witness

The foregoing instrument was acknowledged by me this _____ day of
_____, _____ by _____
who is/are personally known by me or who has/have produced
_____ as identification and who did not
take an oath.

_____ (SEAL)

Notary Public

State of

My Commission Expires:

INDEX

ABOUT THE AUTHOR

Vikki S. Ziegler, Esq. is a practicing attorney of matrimonial law and civil litigation; a television personality known for her commentaries on high-profile celebrity and divorce cases; an active volunteer for various charities; and the innovator of a unique and realistic approach to "divorce management."

Ziegler is a graduate of the University of Rhode Island, where she studied political science, sociology and Spanish, and Quinnipiac College School of Law in Hamden, Connecticut. While a student, she served as judicial law clerk to the Honorable Jerome Hornblaas in the Criminal Part of the State Supreme Court of New York and, in Rhode Island, worked for the Public Defender's office in the Domestic Violence Unit and volunteered at a battered women's shelter.

Following law school graduation in 1998, Ziegler returned to her home state of New Jersey, where she served as a clerk to the Honorable Michael K. Diamond, presiding judge in the Family Division of the Superior Court in Passaic County. While under Diamond's tutelage, she trained as a mediator in small claims and landlord tenant matters, knowledge she has applied to her work as a divorce lawyer. Viewing mediation and settlement as the most beneficial outcome for all, she has successfully settled 99 percent of her cases to date.

In 1999, Ziegler entered private practice, specializing in the areas of matrimonial and civil litigation. She is a member of the Passaic County, Essex County and New Jersey State Bar Associations, as well as a member of the Northern New Jersey and Family Law Inns of Court. Over the course of her career, honors and distinctions have made steady arrival. She was nominated and appointed by the Supreme Court of New Jersey to the District XI Ethics Committee for Passaic County, a four-year term of which she has completed as the Chairperson. In 2006, she was chosen as one of the "Top 40 Lawyers under 40" by the *New Jersey*

Law Journal followed by the same recognition in 2008 by *New Jersey Business News* for her professional excellence and her commitment to her community. In 2011 and 2010, she was recognized as a rising star in *Super Lawyers* magazine and was named a Top 50 Women in Business by *New Jersey Business News* in March 2010. For the past eight years she has served as an Executive Panel Chair in Passaic, Morris and Essex Counties, assisting with recommendations for divorce settlement solutions. She also has volunteered as a moot court judge for Rutgers law students. She is currently an adjunct professor at Fordham Law School, teaching The Art of Drafting Prenuptial Agreements, and Same-Sex Marriage. She was featured in *Image* magazine as the "local spotlight" for her achievements in New Jersey and *The Star Ledger* as an "Active Advocate." She has spoken on various legal topics at symposia and seminars hosted by organizations such as the American Association of Matrimonial Attorneys and the New Jersey Bar Association.

She is often called on to give her expert advice on television, radio and print for the past several years. She is on HLN/CNN, Fox News and Fox Business Channel weekly. She has been on CNBC, MSNBC, Fox 5, Talk Soup on E!, ESPN and many other networks. She is also contributing to top publication such as *People, Ok!, Life and Styles* as well as www.popeater.com, www.thehuffingtonpost.com and www.hollywoodlife.com. She has been quoted in the *NY Times, Washington Times,* momlogic.com, E! news.com, yahoo.com, *NY Post, Daily News* and many others. Her vast media experience has made her a premiere legal expert in her field. She also has coauthored legal articles for *NY Divorce* magazine, *New Jersey Law Journal,* titled "How Can I Keep My Legal Fees Down During My Divorce?" and "Know Your Limits," respectively. She wrote the foreword to Richard Kent's *Mediation vs. Litigation* (December, 2011) and contributed a chapter to the forthcoming *Seven Pearls of Financial Wisdom* by Carol Pepper and Camilla Webster.